Designing School Systems for All Students

Designing School Systems for All Students:

A Tool Box to Fix America's Schools

By
Robert J. Manley, Ph.D.
and
Richard J. Hawkins, Ed.D.

ROWMAN & LITTLEFIELD EDUCATION

A division of

ROWMAN & LITTLEFIELD PUBLISHERS, INC.
Lanham • New York • Toronto • Plymouth, UK

Published by Row.nan & Littlefield Education
A division of Rowman & Littlefield Publishers, Inc.
A wholly owned subsidiary of The Rowman & Littlefield Publishing Group, Inc.
4501 Forbes Boulevard, Suite 200, Lanham, Maryland 20706
http://www.rowmaneducation.com

Estover Road, Plymouth PL6 7PY, United Kingdom

Library of Congress Control Number: 2009939760

ISBN 978-1-60709-373-2 (cloth: alk. paper) — ISBN 978-1-60709-374-9 (pbk: alk.
paper) — ISBN 978-1-60709-375-6 (electronic)

Printed in the United States of America

Contents

Acknowledgments

We would like to thank Kay Manley and Sue Hawkins for their love and support throughout the process of writing this book. Many extra thanks to Kay for helping us edit the manuscript.

Our deepest thanks and gratitude to Tom Koerner and Maera Stratton of Rowman & Littlefield Publishing Group for their unfailing support, expertise, and guidance through the process of bringing this book to fruition.

We acknowledge the hard work and expertise of our colleagues, as well as their dedication and professionalism. We celebrate and illustrate many of our beliefs through their stories and achievements.

The faculty and administration at Southwest Elementary School, Brentwood, New York, who worked on elementary curricula brainstorms—particularly Superintendent Donna Jones, Dr. Aurelia Henriquez, Marilyn Friend-Ituarte, Lisa Robinson, Laura Symons, Nancy Loeber, Donna Plunkett, Jeannette Delgado, Michele Grando, Karen Bonner, Linda Krauthamer, Elizabeth Sheehan, Christine Mercogliano, Jennifer DeMarco, Joan Harney, Erica Stoller, Christine Fitt, and Leslie Bial. We also wish to express our appreciation to Dr. Linda Bausch, Associate Professor of Literacy, of Dowling College, New York, who continues to provide excellent literacy consulting services to Southwest school faculty.

The faculty, staff, and administration at William Floyd Elementary School, Shirley, New York, who created a school environment that valued social and emotional literacy as much as academics.

The members of the William Floyd Character Education committee: Dr. Deborah DeLuca, Peggy Marenghi, Dr. Eugenia Jackolski, Phoebe Arancio, and Lurdes Galarza, whose leadership, talent, capacity for learning, dedication and love for the William Floyd Community were beyond the call of duty.

Jim Lynch, Assistant Principal at West Babylon HS, West Babylon, NY, whose leadership in the Governor's Excellence Awards program helped to form our understanding of systems that work.

Dr. Deepa Sharma, Principal of Shri M. D. Shah Mahila College of Arts and Commerce, Mumbai, India, and Dr. Patel, President of the Board of Trustees, for their collegial support and help in understanding ourselves.

The principal, faculty and staff, who invited us to share a dialogue about education at their pre-school in Xian, China, whose professionalism and whose openness to collaborate and to collegiality impressed us.

We are indebted to Nancy Ordemann for her help formatting our manuscript. She always greeted every revision with enthusiasm and a smile. In addition, we commend the work of our external editor, Rosemarie Webb, who reviewed every line of our manuscript and helped us to clarify our thoughts.

Introduction

If only some individual schools succeed in helping their children learn, many children will be left behind their peers and will be relegated to marginal employment in temporary industries. To some highly effective corporate leaders, quality variations in curriculum, instruction, and student achievement among similar schools seem astoundingly incompetent. After ten years of efforts to reduce variation in student achievement, motivation, and creativity, Bill Gates summed up his impression of American high schools by stating that "American high schools were obsolete" (Gates, 1996).

In 2009, the public high school dropout rates in America's twenty largest cities vary from 50 percent in New York City to 75 percent in Detroit (Cafferty, 2009). Much of the variation in American schools is the result of poorly-structured curriculum, ineffective leadership, poorly-conceived hiring, and staff and student evaluation systems.

In most schools, professional development processes lack focus, goals, and assessment systems, and many school district leaders, governing boards, and superintendents do not believe that they have the money or the capacity to implement curriculum changes that would improve instruction and learning for all children.

In many places, school leaders are content to sustain the current system by facilitating harmonious social interactions. Frequently, harmonious social interactions mean that the superintendent and school board members satisfy their personal dispositions and acquiesce to the most vociferous community members. They maintain their positions of power, yet none seem to really care if students progress as long as their children and the children of their friends do well.

Many school board members report that their boards focus on individual issues that relate to their personal needs and desires such as getting a job for a daughter or son, securing a service contract for a friend or supporter, and achieving credit for positive events in the schools (Chen, 2008). They focus on tax reductions to maintain their power.

Rarely do school board members improve the operations related to the cost of managing facilities or reduce expenditures for supplies, materials, or such services as technology expenses (Bolton, 2006).

In situations repeated more often than one can imagine, school board members and district leaders, with no method to evaluate their performance, satisfy an unreasonable and selfish special-interest group within the community. Many board members perform for the applause of a voting block they believe will help them maintain their power (Feltman, 2003).

They operate similar to local politicians who satisfy particular interests such as parent sports associations or a loud and difficult segment of the community. Often, they miss the main mission of schools and so fail to serve the interest of the students and the larger community.

Board members who ignore the larger mission of the schools, and instead respond to special interests, actually divert the resources of school leaders and distract personnel from the mission of the school. In some cases, individual board members exercise coercive tactics against one or more board members (Feltman, 2003).

Boards that employ a policy governance model benefit from informed public service by their members. Their superintendent, school principals, and the school councils attend to the main mission and goals of the district (Carver, 1997).

At Enron, WorldCom, and the New York Stock Exchange, the governing boards and their chief executives engaged in self-serving activities that were in conflict with the interests of the stockholders. In similar instances, particularly egregious wrongful behaviors occurred in school districts where individuals were involved in deceptions that led to their own failures, indictments, and convictions.

As a result of many selfish acts by public servants, we have a crisis of faith in American enterprises. We know we have descended significantly from the ethos of care, duty, and service that America's forefathers envisioned for a free and good people.

As harmful as unethical behavior is, it is just as disappointing to find some school leaders who ignore the legitimate concerns of parents, that is, that their children master the curriculum. Many educators have been trained to accept large amounts of error among their students. In fact, some students could answer 35 percent of the questions on an exam incorrectly and yet, those students would manage to pass.

Some teachers act as if they were trained to default on their primary responsibility to teach students to learn from their errors, and to achieve mastery of a topic or skill. Often these educators and their leaders accept or adopt a series of excuses that justify failure among the students such as "our students are poor," or "our students speak English as a second language." Such statements are beliefs that foster the status quo and encourage failure.

In some unique cases, affluent districts that have their own challenges are led by board members and educators who compromise on quality and seem satisfied if simply the best and the brightest do well. In these districts, mastery of the curriculum and engaged learning for all students are not the top priorities.

Sadly, in many communities unique successes for a select population capture most of the public's attention. The elite students do well, and the school leaders protect the status quo as normal and desirable.

If you are tired of failure in America's schools, and if you want to change the school system to make it possible for all children to master the curriculum, then read this book.

When the curriculum does not promote exploration, investigation, analysis, synthesis, creativity, and evaluative judgment by all learners, informed educators should recognize that the instructional leadership of the district is weak. In such districts, the board and superintendent have a partnership in mediocrity. They share a failed ethos in which their schools serve the majority and not all children.

In 2009, school districts in America face a growing diverse population of students whose ethical, religious, social and preschool experiences vary more drastically than the values of the entire American workforce. The greater problem for America's schools is not the ethical and professional commitment of its leaders and its governing boards; it is their lack of expertise and training in ethics. It is their lack of training in policy leadership and management selection for complex institutions that is most worrisome.

Most elected officials, most school board members, and most educators want to educate the youth of our nation so that they can be employed in a global economy. Few of them have contemplated how to achieve such a goal. Few have any benchmarks to use to compare how their schools are doing.

We offer comparative examples that school leaders can use to develop curriculum, supervise instruction, and motivate students so that they want to engage in life-long learning.

This book offers clear descriptions of the roles and responsibilities that governing boards and district superintendents and principals must exercise in school districts and their schools. Basic processes that must be in place, constantly practiced, and assessed are described in detail in this book so that any district could improve how it operates its schools.

There are five major principles that must be adhered to if school districts are to ensure that all children make progress in the acquisition of new and necessary knowledge and the mastery of civic virtues required for ademocratic society.

First, schools must have a clear scope and sequence for their curriculum. All teachers should know the curriculum and share its vision for students. Parents and especially the school board should endorse the curricula.

Second, schools must have highly trained ethical and principled leaders who believe in a social democracy where people of different religions, races, cultures, and wealth coexist in a collaborative and shared pursuit of happiness. Educational leaders must be trained to know how to guide learning and the pursuit of happy lives at school. Learning should not be misery. School work should engender pride in all workers (Deming, 1996).

Leaders who can succeed in a democratic society are nurtured. They are prepared for their roles by specific principled beliefs and practices that they learned through their experiences and training. School boards should have policies to develop their teachers and administrators for additional leadership roles in the schools.

Third, effective schools hire leaders who know how to assess and prescribe appropriate interventions to improve how the school is structured and how students learn. Such leaders know how to assess the current reality within their organizations and the mission. They know how to drive progress. They recognize mental models as barriers to necessary change. They use feedback and effective inquiry and dialogue to develop new insights. They formulate a synthesis and a shared vision for future endeavors with all constituents.

Fourth, school districts that achieve high academic success with students who come from a variety of social, cultural, and economic backgrounds hire leaders who know how to motivate faculty and staff. They help teachers adjust their normative practices to the individual students in their classes. They institute reforms that serve the needs of the students and their parents. Their reforms make the jobs of the staff easier. They often return to the staff many tangible and intangible rewards such as the commitment and support of satisfied parents.

Lastly, these effective school systems monitor, assess, develop, and improve all processes within the system. They examine the governance practices of the school board and its senior executives. They try to improve each service center that touches the life of a student, a parent or a resident of the school community.

The entire school system and workforce share a vision of the civic virtues that must be learned, practiced, and protected by all members of the school community for democracy to thrive.

This book lays out a practical approach for boards of education, superintendents, and their staff to implement that leads to more effective schools for all students. The only barrier to effective schools is the will to change, to innovate, and to invent new models of schooling for children of diverse backgrounds.

In this book, we present ways to differentiate the curriculum, to develop leaders, and to improve personnel, instruction, and parent support. We show how to finance learner motivation to meet the needs of each student in unique ways.

We are sharing with you tried and true ways to make a difference in the learning cycle for each student. At the same time, we offer unique ways to overcome the bureaucratic, simplistic testing system anointed by the No Child Left Behind (2001) legislation.

We propose that the methodology available to improve schools begins with a common purpose called a shared vision and curriculum. Several other systems must be in place if schools are to make a difference in the lives of children. Effective school leaders emphasize inquiry and collaboration and lead innovation, effective diagnostics, and prescriptions for student learning.

In effective schools, system thinking serves as a natural tool for continuous improvement. Students engage in learning in a variety of ways. The governing board presents a clear vision, mission, and goals to promote mastery learning among students. Character education captures the spirit of children and enables them to be self-directed learners.

Read our story and see if you agree.

Chapter 1

Getting the Curriculum Right

Curriculum design that includes a scope and sequence analysis is the first step that teachers, principals, and district leaders must take in their journey to build an effective school system. School boards have the responsibility to review the proposed curriculum and to examine its relationship to the mores of the community. Boards should adopt a challenging curriculum that engages the intellectual capacity of its students and promotes a desire to contribute to the school community.

Marzano (2003) noted that even school districts that devote time to curricula development pay little attention to the implemented curricula. In fact, the published curricula receive the lion's share of attention, while what teachers actually teach, what children actually learn, and how their outcomes on standard tests align with published curricula are rarely well-evaluated.

The reason that so few districts analyze their curricula outcomes is that very few school boards or school councils have a methodology that requires a public and open evaluation of curricula and student learning. There are few school districts with effective methods to evaluate curricula. Schools boards do not know how to rely on their school principals and their teaching staff to present curricula evaluations. Most methods are cumbersome and impractical. Often they don't make much of a difference because they focus on inputs and ignore the outcomes that count.

Because of the inordinate reliance on standardized testing in the United States, many curricula assessments ignore the contributions that the professional staff can make in the analysis of the value, comprehensiveness, and continuity of the curricula. They simply report percentages of students at proficiency as curricula outcomes.

Frequently, curricula in school districts are purchased from textbook publishers who attest that their textbooks are aligned to the state testing standards. Teachers and principals are eliminated from the process of textbook evaluation and curricula development.

Professional training is relegated to textbook company representatives teaching teachers how to use the text and its assessments. No brain power among the teachers is expected, and their ability to diagnose learning needs and prescribe appropriate instructional methods for their students is discounted.

So many barriers to professional involvement of teachers exist as part of the normal environment in schools that one must conclude that either teachers are perceived as untrustworthy vehicles to deliver information, or they are considered incompetent. As a result, teachers do not share in the determination of what they should teach and how they should assess their own performance.

In other words, in many school districts, teachers are systematically denied the basic rights of professionals. They are not responsible for their own work, and they are not expected to assess its quality.

Certainly, hospital boards and senior executives know how to assess divisions and staff contributions to the hospital's mission while maintaining the professionalism of the staff. Many hospital professionals participate in their own development and assessment processes. School boards and their senior executives should be able to perform the same executive actions as most hospital executives do.

The problem for boards of education and school councils is that they typically do not have the training to develop the professional skills of teachers and administrators. They rely on administrators and teachers to develop their own skills in curricula design and evaluation through an individual and disconnected self-selection process.

Boards have been conditioned by the media to blame employees for student failure. Most curricula evaluations in school districts rely on state testing programs and textbook publishers to determine how effective curricula and instruction are. Competent boards engage in reflective practice and continuous learning. They are aware of how much training they and the staff need to do before they try to design better school systems.

Conflicts of interest exist for state and textbook-company-driven assessments because the systems feed each agency's need for acceptable levels of success. As a result, the instructional practices in classroom after classroom reflect an institutional demand that teachers prepare students for the tests. In the United States, why do we have fifty separate, distinct and unequal methods to assess school progress for individual states? Are the curricula that different?

Politicians enjoy whipping the schools for failure, and publishers enjoy funding from state departments of education that endorse their testing programs as assessments of student failures. The tests are not designed to assess student growth in learning.

Every educator in the country knows that the assessment of learning occurs over time and individually from student to student on similar and disparate measures. Time to master a discipline or a subject may vary from months to years especially for students with learning disabilities and second-language issues.

If the United States wants to assess student learning levels, the American Council for Testing (ACT) has national exams that assess the level of knowledge that students have acquired in English, Mathematics, History, and Science. The federal government could pay for all eighth- and eleventh-graders to take these exams. Such a testing system would provide national norms and an annual snapshot of where student academic performance fell across the nation.

As Edwards Deming (1994) noted, testing would not improve the system. National tests would provide a still-life portrait of students at a moment of time. Why test? If the President and leaders in the federal government want to improve school performance across the nation, they have to reward student achievement and the communities and staff who contribute to the desired student success.

One way to reward students and schools for success is to have students participate in national achievement testing programs. Schools should not be faulted for student performance. Schools should be rewarded. Success should be the focus. Political scientist Deborah Stone (2001) observed that when organizations decide to count the number of occurrences of a particular phenomenon, the counting practice leads to finding more of the phenomenon. Therefore, she notes that a paradoxical result is that if one counts negative events, such as failures, the organization will find more failures. In the United States, we need to count and reward student success.

One of the simplest ways to reward schools and communities for the success of their students is to provide a federal grant of $10,000 dollars to any school system in which a student achieved a 4 or 5 on the annual Advanced Placement exams. Ninety percent of the grant could pay the state retirement system for teacher and employee pension debts accrued by the district for that year, and reduce the local tax payers' bill. Ten percent of the award could provide additional staff development for the next year.

In such a reward system, the people who have invested in the children would benefit as well as the employees. School boards in districts with significant growth in scholar awards could share a special stipend with all employees as part of the awards program.

How do state standard tests, measuring yearly progress of different student groups, fit into this awards program? They do not.

School board members, school leaders, parents, and students should treat all state testing results as politically-based propaganda, and instead must focus on local, teacher driven assessments to adjust instruction and intervention plans for students. National exams that incorporate criterion-based assessment methodologies would help reveal the level of knowledge a student has in a particular subject. Such results can inform employers and colleges about a student's readiness for work or higher education.

As most employers and college admission officers know, tests do not predict a student's goals, desire for success, or ability to strive and succeed in college and in a career

School boards, parents, taxpayers, administrators, and teachers do not have to wait for state and federal governments to establish standards of performance. The vehicles already exist. Local school leaders should exercise their professional duties and implement a fair and accurate testing model so that student academic performance can be fairly and validly assessed across the nation.

One should not confuse performance on a valid national criterion-referenced test with indicators of future success at work or college. Even the best tests will not predict more than small amounts of success among college students. Tests do not measure the determination and drive of the student, nor the quality of the interpersonal exchanges between faculty and students and among students themselves.

At work, there are few tests that will predict the successes of employees to a valuable level of certainty. Tests indicate what the test-takers have learned and not what they might do with the right supervision, training, instruction, peer support and motivation to succeed.

Nevertheless, unless superintendents and school boards lead the way and change how testing drives instruction, our schools will continue to reflect a bureaucratic and growing mechanistic environment. Drilling and practicing for tests is poisonous to the joy of learning and to the quality instruction that students deserve.

Schools with high rates of poverty suffer the most because their students continue to experience the drudgery of test preparation. These poor students lack true learning activities, and their dropout rates continue to climb (Bossert, 2008; Christie, 2009; Fulton, 2009).

Districts must reject teaching to tests and adopt a viable curriculum to motivate students to stay in school. They must offer students opportunities to develop leadership. Students need to explore knowledge and expand decision-making skills for full citizenship. They want to have a sense of belonging to their school and feel like they are part of a community (Sergiovanni, 1994; Glasser, 1990). For these reasons, schools must have viable curriculum (Marzano, 2003).

BUILDING VIABLE CURRICULUM

One method associated with effective school boards that improves student achievement and supports high satisfaction among residents and employers is an annual review of curricula designs, their costs and historical outcomes. School boards can adopt this methodology in a sequential format by imposing a four-year cycle on all curriculum reviews (Burak, 2006).

Few school boards know if an annual planned review of curriculum is difficult or even a costly operation. Even fewer boards know how it works. School boards that make a difference in the learning cycle of children require that their administrators present an annual report that explains the sequence of selected curricula from grade to grade, how the curricula build skills one upon another, the costs, and the actual performance of the students on approved outcome measurements.

Outcome data on approved measurements are collected annually in these effective districts so that student growth and improvements can be identified on criterion-referenced tests. Such data are shared publicly with the school council and the board of education.

In these effective school districts and schools, long-term and annual curricula assessment is a public process in which school administrators annually present a thorough analysis of outcomes regarding at least four distinct curricula.

The critical ingredient in curriculum assessment is that leaders, community constituents and educators agree about the sequence and content of the curricula through a public review of state standards. School leaders should demonstrate how curricula are aligned and exceed state standards for academic performance.

Curricula should have a clear purpose that meets the expectations of the community for its students. School boards should adopt curricula publicly and ensure that the content meets the district's mission, previously established by the school board.

Unless the school board adopts and publishes curricula, teachers and administrators are subject to diverse attacks about any topic that is taught which may violate the sensibilities of some segment of a local constituency. A typical curricula evaluation schedule follows a planned sequence such as the one we present in Table 1.1.

Table 1.1. Sequence for Curriculum Evaluation and Improvement

Time	Curriculum Review	Costs	Benefits to Students
Year One	Language Arts Social Studies Music Arts	Total dollars for salaries & benefits	Outcome measures that include tests and other selected feedback measures
Year Two	Math Science Educational Technology Home and Career		
Year Three	Foreign Language Business Education Occupational Education Special Education/ Advanced Placement		

Year Four	Counseling/Guidance/
	    Social Services
	Reading/Speech Services
	Co-curricular and
	    Extra-curricular Activities
	Learning Intervention
	    Services		

The public adoption and evaluation of curricula by the governing board of a school system delivers a message to all employees and residents that the content of the programs and the outcomes that students achieve are important.

Designing a curriculum is a precise academic and professional task that requires extensive knowledge of the subject matter and the principles of curriculum design. The cognitive, social and emotional development of children must be delineated clearly in effective curricula (Santos, 2009). Curricula for schools should have a thematic structure that focuses upon knowledge that a student must acquire within a subject matter.

For each subject theme, clear statements of what the student is expected to do as a result of instruction should be expressed. Assessments of a student's mastery of the topic and performance expectations should be expressed in the curricular outline in such areas as homework, tests, portfolios, projects, research papers, and experiments.

Curricula should be structured within an appropriate pattern and follow a sequence that adheres to material content such as chronological events in history, a logical sequence in mathematics or the psychological development of the student in the humanities. Table 1.2 presents the principles of curriculum design that work for students.

Table 1.2. Principles of Curriculum Design

Purpose	*Process*
Theme:	*Assessments:*
Organize topics within a theme	Homework expands theme application
Expectations reveal student capacity	Tests, portfolios and presentations
Organization:	*Curriculum Options:*
Themes and topics follow a pattern	Chronological order
Expectations frame levels of operations	Logical order
Expectations set high standards	Psychological order

Principles of curriculum design have four variables that must be considered. First, the curriculum must have purpose. It should have clear learning goals set in a planned scope and sequence that guides developmental learning. The curriculum should be organized with expectations for student performance in terms of cognitive, social and emotional development of good citizens. Assessments and criteria to measure student learning should be explicitly stated in the curriculum. Finally, the curriculum should be organized according to three options: chronological themes, logical and psychological sequences.

For instance, a teacher should approach Shakespeare's Romeo and Juliet very differently in grade nine with thirteen-year-old students than s/he would with twelfth-grade students. The psychological, emotional, and social experiences of the two student groups, one pre-adolescent and the other pre-adult, would be quite different. The two groups would require different expectations for interpretation, perspective, synthesis, and evaluation.

Math and science curricula require sequential development of specific knowledge before new knowledge can be acquired. Such logically-organized curricula have natural sequences that require some pre-knowledge. Designers of science and math curricula recognize the interdependence of a variety of knowledge in these subjects.

History, literature, music, art, and languages seem to serve a common purpose, and students would benefit from some planned integration of the themes and topics within and across the grade levels. For instance, when music and art teachers design their curricula, do they work with the grade-level classroom teachers to synchronize similar skills and historical events so that the classroom topics and expectations for student performance are integrated across the subjects? More importantly, how do teachers express their expectations for students? Do the teachers in a school share a common language and understanding about the structure of the curricula? In our experience, it is rare for teachers to have a common language and understanding about the structure of their curriculum.

As recently as May 21, 2008, Bob Manley conducted a workshop for principals in which fifty high school principals were asked if anyone had read or was familiar with Benjamin Bloom's book, *All Our Children Learning*, or *Bloom's Taxonomy*, and if so, how it could be used to structure curriculum and engage students more deeply in critical thinking. The response was that they were a bit more familiar with Grant Wiggins and Jay McTighe's book, *Understanding by Design* (2001). Yet, they had little practical knowledge of how to apply either theory to curricular design at their schools.

Bloom (1981) offers a clear structure under which teachers can design their curricula. He emphasizes the cognitive domain within a student's learning capacity and suggests that the affective domain supports engaged learning. Wiggins and McTighe stress three aspects of cognition and three emotive expressions that should occur within all curricular designs for understanding.

Teachers should design curriculum statements in such clear language that anyone reading the curriculum would be able to identify the topic and theme to be learned. The level of cognition that the student was expected to achieve and for which s/he would be tested should be boldly stated. Curriculum should engage students far beyond the simple cognitive tasks of recall and interpretation. Children should be prepared to apply knowledge so they can create knowledge.

Bloom's Taxonomy for engaged learning provides teachers and all other curriculum developers with clear action words that describe behaviors students perform to demonstrate mastery of a topic. By knowing the cognitive level at which a student is expected to perform, teachers can individuate instruction seamlessly within a single classroom.

Wiggins and McTighe provide additional guiding principles that teachers can use to describe their expectations for students within a single subject. They introduce the self-reflective and emotional aspects of curriculum design and ask that teachers plan to engage students in a holistic manner.

For our part, we recommend that all teachers and curriculum designers employ, in their curricular outlines, the performance-based action words that Bloom, Wiggins and McTighe suggest.

Whenever teachers write curriculum for children or adults, they must remember that students need to know what is expected of them. The curriculum should not read like a lesson plan or an outline to guide teacher instructional practices. Curriculum should focus on what the learner can do.

Teachers should be the architects of the curriculum. Administrators should be the evaluators of the design. School boards should judge the quality of the student outcomes. School boards have yet another curricular responsibility:

Table 1.3. Bloom's Taxonomy Contrasted with Wiggins and McTighe

Bloom's Taxonomy (1981)	Wiggins and McTighe (2001)
Cognitive Domain	Knowledge
Understand (recall)	Can explain
Comprehend (explain)	Can interpret
Apply (demonstrate)	Can apply
Analyze (contrast)	Can see perspective
Synthesize (connect)	Can empathize
Evaluate (judge)	Can self assess

to adopt quality curriculum plans that meet the standards of their community and state.

In Table 1.3 we contrast curricula expressions from Bloom with those from Wiggins and McTighe to demonstrate the constructs that should underlie all curricula designs.

In our work with teachers, we have learned how open they are to learning about the design of curriculum, and how devoted they are to enhancing the quality of thinking, reading, research, and writing among their students.

Teachers can create the performance-based statements that measure their students' cognitive, social, and emotional mastery of the curriculum. Teachers who focus on mastery expectations, as these teachers do, motivate students to achieve. Notice how engaging the mastery assessments are for the students in the literacy curriculum statements for kindergarten and first grade. See how they require active learning.

Students who experience high curriculum expectations are motivated by the content of the curriculum. They respond to the context of the teacher expectations for multiple levels of cognition and empathetic performance. They enjoy and respond to active verbs that cause them to be agents of their own learning.

In Tables 1.4 and 1.5, we present two examples of sequence and scope of English language arts curricula that incorporate instructional framework and performance expectations for students in the same outline.

Table 1.4 presents kindergarten literacy curriculum for reading and writing in terms of curriculum and student performance expectations that extend across the continuum of cognitive and social-emotional developmental processes that all curricula should contain.

The performance expectations focus on what students can do as a result of instruction. They are statements that provide measurable behavior that the students can demonstrate. Teaching impacts student cognitive and dispositional levels in this literacy curriculum. Mastery applications of new literacy knowledge at kindergarten and first grade are expressed in terms that all children can exhibit with practice and help.

Table 1.4. Kindergarten Curriculum with Student Performance Expectations

	Student Performance	
Expectations Curriculum	*Read*	*Write*
Phonemic awareness		
Master anguage rocessing levels through E3	Build words with sounds & objects	Segment sentences with lines
Identify and create rhyme	Word sort by sounds	Fill-in sound box with letter
Print awareness		
Distinguish the difference between letters, numbers, words, and pictures	Explain letter, number, word, and picture	Sequence words in sentence strips
Learn concept of left and right		Sequence pictures of a story
Demonstrate knowledge of left to right progression of print/top to bottom/ front cover, back cover/title page		
Develop concept of word/ tracking print	Dictate a story	Interpret a dictation
Alphabet recognition and phonics		
Recognize and name all uppercase and lowercase manuscript letters of the alphabet	Explain upper & lower case	Write a personal thought
Develop sound/symbol association	Analyze letters	
Background knowledge and vocabulary		
Develop A.R.L. language of instruction	Retell a story with new characters, setting, or ending	Predict what comes next in a story
Learn the meaning of new words and use them in their own speech		
Connect life experiences to ideas and books		
Engage in meaningful conversation		
Fluency		
Speak in complete sentences		
Recognize their own first and last names	Build a class list of new and illustrated words	Use new words in context
Recognize sight words from Macmillan/ McGraw-Hill in isolation and in text	Read aloud familiar stories	Reread student experience charts about texts
Comprehension		
Derive meaning from text	Sing songs and recite poems connected to print	Connect music and art to stories, poems, songs and events
Retell a story		
Match pictures to text		
Sequence the events of the story		
Identify story elements	Converse about the meaning of words and ideas in songs, pictures, stories and events	

(Continued)

Table 1.4. *(Continued)*

	Student Performance	
Expectations Curriculum	*Read*	*Write*
Motivation to read		
Develop an interest in reading	Read silently	Share ideas,
Become familiar with nursery rhymes		feelings,surprises, and important elements of silent reading or picture gazing

Table 1.5 presents the first-grade literacy curriculum and student performance expectations for reading and writing. Notice how the empathetic level expands at this grade and how students are expected to perform with greater self-awareness.

Imagine asking a tenured teacher, with this level of curricula autonomy, to prepare students for a test through weeks of drill and practice. These teachers would rightly ignore such mechanistic expectations and continue to teach above the expectations of the tests. Their students would perform above the norms of the test too.

How do school leaders guarantee that teachers obtain the freedom to teach, and that students enjoy the delights of learning from an informed and autonomous professional teacher? Teachers and administrators must work together to inform school boards how to use policy to guide a professional staff in the development of quality curricula.

Teachers must have the autonomy to engage students in important discoveries about language, words, and mythologies as well as scientific, mathematical and historical phenomenon.

Teachers and administrators should demand that their school boards require the faculty and administration to present and justify the scope and sequence of curricula in a planned and developmental process. School boards that coordinate planned and public sessions where administrators and teachers evaluate curricula and current teaching practices, in terms of student achievement, change their low expectations for teachers and school leaders. They learn how complex teaching is.

When boards of education understand the complexity of teaching, they comprehend how hard teachers work to help students learn. They see the need for new training and curricular development. The frequent result of placing a public spotlight on teaching and learning is that all constituents learn what they did not know. They learn that the presenters are competent and able to evaluate their own work. They learn to listen.

Table 1.5.   First Grade Curriculum and Student Performance Expectations

	Performance	
Expectations Curriculum	*Read*	*Write*
Phonemic awareness		
Continue to develop Language Processing levels Letter and sound manipulation (changing beginning and ending sounds)	Explain how words sound the same and spell differently	Pick five pairs of words on the computer that sound the same and spell differently.
Phonics		
Read comprehensive list of short and long vowel keys Apply knowledge of keys to decode words Develop word attack skills	Decode words in context of a story	Demonstrate decoding and spelling
Background knowledge and vocabulary		
Develop A.R.L. Language of Instruction Learn the meaning of new words and use them in their own speech Connect life experiences to books Engage in meaningful conversation Speak in complete sentences	Interpret a story Empathize with people in a news story	Create a new character in a story Write a note to help a child
Fluency		
Recognize sight words from Macmillan McGraw-Hill in isolation and in text Use punctuation and inflection when reading aloud	Read with emotion and inflection	Punctuate a sentence using question mark and commas
Comprehension		
Derive meaning from text Retell a story Distinguish between fact/fiction Sequence the events of the story Identify story elements Interpret graphic organizers Engage in meaningful discussion about a book Ask questions in response to text	Make a judgment about a person in a story Assess what you learned from a reading	Organize a graphic design of people, places and events Predict what might come next in the text
Motivation to read		
Develop an interest in reading from a variety of genres Become familiar with fairy tales Select appropriate independent readings	Justify a personal choice for reading Interpret the moral of a fable.	Identify and explain favorite readings

The scope and content of district curricula should be presented to the board of education in public session. School board members should require that their educational leaders justify the scope and content of the proposed curricula. Teachers and curricular leaders should demonstrate how such curricula are aligned with and exceed national and state standards for learning at various grade levels.

Student performance on local and state exams should be reported by grade level for males and females and ethnic majorities and minorities within a school system and a school. Educational leaders, teachers and school board members as well as community members should be able to see and monitor student success in the major academic subjects from year to year. These transparent leadership actions are the foundation of an open and continuously-improving school system.

We are concerned that the United States does not have a national standard for high school leaving exams as many of our competing nations have. We are concerned that student results on national exams are viewed as school-related measurements of quality when in fact they are individual measurements of the total life experience of students.

National standard exams do nothing more than assess the educational health of the nation's high school graduates as a group. They present a position for each student within the group performance. They are not important or highly accurate predictors of future success.

Nevertheless, we believe that a method for students to acquire accurate information about their academic standing compared to their peers across the nation would encourage students to take high school seriously.

If school boards were to adopt the national criterion-referenced examinations of the ACT as exit exams from the eighth and twelfth grades, they would provide a high and uniform standard for every child in school at grades eight and twelve to use for self-assessment. At the high school level, such exams could be the standard for exit exams. In other words, a student's scores on the ACT exams would be the published record of the student's academic achievement available on the high school diploma.

In an ACT assessment system, passing the required courses for the high school diploma and any state standard exams would enable the student to graduate with a diploma. Low scores on the ACT exams would permit a student to repeat the test at its next administration and/or take additional coursework until the student becomes twenty-one years of age.

Local school boards would do their graduates a favor by establishing a national standard for them, and at the same time, offer them motivation to succeed. Boards should not use the exams to assess curriculum, teaching and learning in a school or to compare schools. Such comparisons would be false and a misuse of the test because they would assume the all the students started school at the same place in the learning curve.

The exams should be viewed as a school's Magnetic Resonating Imaging (MRI) for students. The ACT exams in a school exit system serve as helpful visuals to assess learning needs that remain within a student or group of students. For some students, the exams would note a need for more time in high school. For other students, the exams would indicate readiness for work or higher education. School district boards of education could provide their students, parents, and teachers with accurate and helpful guidance about the status of student learning by offering ACT exams for all students.

To assess curricula, superintendents and school board members need a separate and more complex methodology. School board members should expect that their educational leaders and other school administrators can accurately present the annual cost to implement a curriculum. Cost is a critical factor for public schools, and schools that employ leaders and supervisors that do not know the costs of personnel, their benefits and their training, and the materials, software, hardware, and textbooks that they use to teach a particular curriculum do not have the information they need to assess the impact of their investments of public money.

Supervisors and school administrators should be able to discuss how many students perform at the proficient and mastery levels in the curricula under investigation. They should present any additional benefits that they can describe for student participation in curricular and co-curricular programs. They should have multiple artifacts to present student mastery of the curriculum.

Student and parent feedback loops should be utilized annually to investigate curricular and co-curricular benefits. Recipients of the curricula should have a way to report what they believe are important and highly valued activities such as field trips, technology applications, and community-service programs.

Feedback about the many school events that motivate students to learn, to develop leadership skills, and to stay in school should be incorporated into all program evaluations.

In the final analysis, well-educated students who do not reflect democratic values are not an asset to a democratic society. When students give service to one another, to the elderly, or to the community at large, they demonstrate the quality of the adult citizen they will become. More than any test score on a state or local exam, the ways students serve others, cooperate and formulate decisions predict the quality of citizens they will be.

Although multiple levels of cognitive content, sequence, and emotional-social performance are important, the most critical issue for American public schools is not the content of their academic curricula. If all of the academic expectations in a state's or district's curricula were mastered by the students and the students did not have the character to use their knowledge as productive citizens, what good would their education be?

School boards, superintendents, and principals have to take a leadership role in developing the civic values that will be practiced in the district schools. Those civic values should be identified in cooperation with parents, and should be pervasive experiences in all curricula within the schools.

In one New York district that we investigated, community representatives, educators, instructional support staff, business leaders, parents, and school board members joined together to determine the civic values that all staff would teach and practice. The school board used feedback from the community, school personnel, and students to assess the quality and impact of their civic virtue programs. The five civic values that this community selected as essential to their survival and to the success of their stated mission were as follows: Respect for oneself, Respect for others, Integrity, Accepting responsibility for one's own actions, and Giving service to one's community.

In another district, Deluca and Hawkins (2006) initiated a school-wide effort to inculcate civic virtues among students and staff in one elementary school during a two-year period. After two years, feedback indicated that civic virtues held meaning for students, parents, teachers, and instructional support staff in the school because they practiced them daily.

Vandalism and violence between students declined in this school as the new civic virtues became the norm. Parents, employees, and students in this public school acted differently under the influence of these virtues. They no longer accepted excuses for student academic failure, misbehavior, and lack of involvement in the school.

They adopted a philosophy that negative and harmful behaviors in school were the natural responses people made to a poorly-designed educational system. They changed the learning and recognition system to achieve the good results that they wanted.

In another district in New Jersey, faculty, administrators, and parents determined that they would have an inclusive classroom environment for students with handicapping conditions. Students with severe to moderate learning difficulties were treated with empathy and acceptance by administrators, faculty, students, and parents. The effects of leadership and caring values were evident in this school system where every employee was trained to work with students with a variety of handicapping conditions.

We observed a student, who had been ostracized by her peers in a neighboring district because of her severely delayed speech and communicative issues, accepted by her teachers in her new high school. She was offered a multiplicity of ways to participate in the curricula that challenged her to perform effectively in spite of her disabilities. During her four years at the school, her depressed level of confidence that she had acquired in her previous school dissipated. Her confidence grew in her ability to communicate with her peers and elicit a positive response.

At this high school, we observed that she volunteered to participate in many new opportunities in curricular and co-curricular activities. As she progressed, many additional options to engage in student activities were extended to her. She responded positively to new offers to interact with her peers and grew comfortable in those settings. She learned to master their requirements.

We saw her invited by teachers to participate in after-school theater productions and other activities. We witnessed the star of the annual musical invite her and two of her classmates to the cast party at his home. We saw this inclusive value system exhibited by parents who invited this student and her classmates to enjoy a day at a pool party and an overnight pajama party.

When it came time to set up roommates for the annual band trip, senior students met with teacher advisors to ensure all students had classmates with whom they would share accommodations. Senior students were in charge of the rooms and extended invitations to all underclass men and women. In every instance, students felt selected and wanted in the room assignments that they received. These invitations would never have been extended in her home district.

The power of inclusive values that were publicized and monitored by the school board, administrators, instructional and instructional support staff were physically evident to us in the words of this sixteen-year-old girl: "In my other school, I was alone. Here, people are kind."

Professional educators and trustees of schools should reflect on the pain of isolation and alienation that teenagers can suffer for religious beliefs or practices, for their size, color, learning difficulties or social weaknesses. Think of the life experience a child endures when the school culture, which is a living curriculum, supports exclusivity rather than a caring and inclusive belief system.

The most critical cultural curriculum that school districts should assess annually is the culture of care in its schools as perceived by the staff, teachers, students, and parents (Stone, 1996; Caputo, 2007). Significant variances in the perceptions of students or their parents about the quality of care at the school should be causes of concern for administrators, school council members, and school board members.

Districts should use trend and benchmark data to compare the local district to neighboring and regional high performing districts. Effective school districts use benchmarks to examine their own performance and to develop future performance goals. All district employees should serve on teams that have true responsibility for student performance. They should have clear goals and a method to evaluate their own work. Criteria for success should be set for each professional team at the outset of the year.

Districts should have their own internal curricula goals. Administrators should assess progress annually and report to the school board in public session. In the most effective schools, school administrators see themselves as professionals who partner with professional teachers much as radiologists work with surgeons.

When teachers serve as partners with administrators in student learning plans, they diagnose student needs, prescribe and treat. Administrators affirm or challenge the effectiveness of the outcomes. Teachers share with students the adventure of learning together. They work in teams of similar subject and grade-level assignments and assess learning.

Administrators support and share in teacher efforts to find the best procedures and technology to advance learning among the students and the faculty. Students should not and need not be the only learners in a school.

Long ago, effective schools abandoned the factory model of the nineteenth century where bosses controlled workers and focused on time management issues and end-of-the-line testing of product quality (Callahan, 1962). Effective schools focus on quality curriculum, important student and parent feedback, professional development of teachers, and multiple assessments of student growth. They pay little heed to standard high-stakes test results.

How can districts operate at this high level of transparency and accountability? Is it difficult? Of course it is difficult because it requires highly-trained school board members, superintendents, administrators, instructional and instructional support staff who understand their role as members of a social agency in a democratic society.

Governing boards that achieve their goals use policy and public evaluations as guiding hands to steer their fleet of schools. Rather than allow individual charisma or influence of some board members, instructional leaders or superintendents to drive instruction, personnel are guided by policy, clear values, and professional norms.

Effective school boards and school decision-making councils hold their employees accountable for proper planning, execution and achievement of the mission and the learning objectives that they oversee. Respect for the autonomy of the professionals is pervasive. The professional educators hold themselves to high levels of accountability, and monitor how well they achieve their shared vision and mission.

Professional educators expect to appear before school boards to demonstrate their achievements and to outline plans to meet the ever-changing needs of their students. Sadly, professional models of governance and leaders who know how to implement them are not prevalent in America's schools.

School boards need to learn how to deliver necessary benefits to their students, their young adults, homeowners, residents, and business owners in the district. To ignore any element of the school community is a failure of leadership. Such a default usually results in multiple failures for the entire system. If segments of a community are ignored, diverse constituents will fight for recognition and disrupt the board's planning process and teamwork. Internecine warfare destroys teamwork and creates dysfunctional systems.

Districts and schools with extensive or even continuous turnover at the top among school board members and senior executives tend to be contentious environments with unusually high costs and very little productivity. Such school systems put out fires, respond to continuous small crises, and rarely establish long-term plans.

School districts with high turnover rates among their school leaders rarely assess how they are doing in terms of the learning curriculum and student achievement in a public forum.

Normal districts with relative harmony among their board members and executive leaders tend to ignore the examination of curricula too. The costs and benefits analyses of school programs for students, the community and its employers even in the best of districts tend to be reduced to simple accountability measures of tax rate increases and passing rates on statewide normative tests (Burak, 2006).

Few school districts know how to conduct gain-score analysis for students in ways that parents and employers could use to recognize how much growth the children achieved in comparison to their relative normalized position on tests from one benchmark year to another. Few school district leaders and school board members understand their proper role in the adoption and evaluation of curricular outcomes.

In addition, diplomas do not have benchmark scores for graduation exams listed on them in the United States. Employers cannot assess the level of mastery that a student achieved on important subjects related to employment in a particular craft or profession. In the first decade of the twenty-first century in the United States, minimal competency is sufficient for a high school diploma, and employers rarely ask for more than a diploma.

In some professions and large corporations, personnel officers examine grades and grade point averages on a transcript knowing full well that they cannot compare the grades from a transcript at one school to another school. They use scores to make political decisions about candidates selected for interviews. They do not have an equitable standard to compare job applicants.

The interview and past history of the applicant comprise the criteria for employment. In some enlightened companies, tests have been purchased and administered to applicants to assess specific skills and dispositions that employers seek.

In America, the kindergarten-to-twelfth-grade education system remains disconnected from the world of college, productive work, and good citizenship.

The No Child Left Behind (2001) legislation in the United States permits each of the fifty states to set individual standards and to design distinctive tests. The variations in scope, difficulty, and cognitive skills among these state examinations make the scores incomparable across the states.

If school boards selected the ACT as exit exams for grade twelve, school districts could publish percentages of students with scores in four quartiles on the exit exams. A national standard testing system would provide school boards and communities with a common reference point for academic performance. If school boards adopted the ACT Standard for high school exit exams, the national standards would not be under the auspices of a federal bureaucracy.

There would not be a bureaucratic standard to destroy the diversity and productivity of Americans. Diversity and productivity go hand-in-hand and must be preserved as one of America's greatest assets (Page, 2008). School boards can lead the way.

School boards do not have to wait for the federal government to create national criterion-referenced achievement tests. They can act now and adopt their own national standards for performance for their districts' leaving exams. The American College Testing service already provides ACT Exams for eighth and eleventh grade that could be used as exiting exams.

Exiting exams for eighth and eleventh grade would encourage students and parents to assess where a particular student's strengths were in comparison to the national sample. Parents could act on that academic information in such a way that an individual student and family could make an informed decision regarding how he or she should pursue future studies and prepare for employment and citizenship.

Since it is unlikely that the federal government or the department of education will take the necessary steps to implement a national assessment program for all schools, innovative school boards that are willing to act should act and protect America's productivity.

Teachers in local districts and teachers in benchmark districts could develop, in a collaborative process, diagnostic procedures to identify strengths and weaknesses on the new exit exams and devise ways to increase student mastery.

Schools could print aggregate scores for student groups and performance percentiles for selected valued subjects on the students' diploma. Students would know immediately how they ranked compared to their peers, and more importantly, what percentage of the expected knowledge that they should have acquired actually had been mastered.

Under current laws in most states, students whose scores were so low that they were not able to demonstrate proficiency in required subjects could remain in school until twenty-one years of age. Some students would take advantage of this option and obtain as much academic and civic skill and knowledge as they could. Students could use their scores on exiting exams as competitive reference points in their pursuit of employment.

Employers and colleges might come to respect these assessments as indicators of promise more reliable than other national or statewide assessments since they would be representative of national and independent performance standards that were not attached to political expedient endeavors.

If local school systems select ACT exams as exit exams, and if the federal government rewards school systems for students who achieve a 4 or 5 on the Advanced Placement exams, the federal government could remove itself from the testing business and, instead, enter the stimulus business for education.

An ACT-driven assessment system would prevent having a few select textbook publishers serve as testing agencies, with all the conflicts of interest that inbreeding creates. Valued and experienced agencies like the College Board and the American Council on Testing would be employed as the nation's independent testing agencies.

The pressure to teach to a test would be removed by the style and design of advanced placement and ACT exams that measure cognitive operations like writing and thinking, applications of knowledge in selected and valued scenarios, and the ability to substantiate a judgment and empathize with diverse people.

Another benefit of a change in the testing systems of the United States would be that districts could cease their pursuit of minimal competencies and seek mastery-level performance from all of their students. Other respected performance-based exams in selected measurements could be added to the school board's student assessment plan, such as exams in cosmetology, county trade licenses, pilot license, and civil service exams that students ought to be able to submit as part of their exiting exam scores to achieve their high school diploma.

Each district should have the autonomy to decide how to best serve the population of the community, and at the same time develop mastery-level performance in the graduates for English, World History, American History, Mathematics, and Life Science.

In the school and student accountability system that we propose, students present their scores on a common standard that has been determined at the national level. Simultaneously, they exhibit their scores on local, standard assessments that show employers, districts and state departments of education measurements that assess the quality of their learning experiences.

By publishing a student's performance on a diploma in a few uniform academic tests and other locally selected measurements, school districts can save many dollars in testing and test preparation programs.

Students and their parents as well as teachers and administrators would share more equitably in the responsibility for the results that students achieve if the school board selected the ACT as exit exams for grades eight and twelve. At the same time, a streamlined testing program permits more money for teachers and equipment. With more highly trained teachers and support staff, students might continuously improve what they know and what they can do as citizens in a local community.

The system we have in America in 2009 is broken and no amount of testing at grades three to eight will improve a failed design (Gates, 1996). The basic understanding of system theory is missing in the legislation of No Child Left Behind (NCLB) because NCLB assumes that authorities can test excellence into a system.

All system experts understand that excellent systems produce excellence, and no amount of testing can improve a poorly designed system (Deming, 1994; Senge, 2000).

Testing children after they experienced a system for one or more years would confirm what the system produced and would not improve the process at all. To improve a system designed to educate children with diverse needs, the system would have to have enormous flexibility. Small class sizes of fifteen students in kindergarten to grade two would be essential to a literacy program that intended to have all students be independent readers by grade three.

Confident leaders and highly trained teachers, who could differentiate instruction according to the needs of each child, would have to be hired. Their skills would have to be developed continuously as diversity expanded within a school population.

Our school leaders understand that teachers who differentiate instruction within the normal class and its normal hours also go beyond the regular school day in tutorials with children. Approximately 24 percent of US students need more intensive attention than teachers can deliver in a classroom with twenty-four students. Schools need sufficient flexibility to respond to students in need. Tutorials managed by teachers for their own students on a weekly basis offer the foundations of academic flexibility and differentiated instruction.

Teachers master differentiated instructional techniques through intensive training in diagnostics and multiple learning applications, curricular design knowledge, innovation, experimentation, and the proper use of technology. Such teaching skills become the norm in a school where administrators make continuous efforts to develop their staff.

Without specific and direct efforts by school leaders to develop differentiated teaching skills among teachers, teachers follow the path of least resistance and teach to the average skill level of the group or they teach to the test.

At one time, the scope and sequence of a learning plan was termed a curriculum. In 2008, after NCLB legislation, curriculum has largely become a test preparatory program. Teachers want to return to the days when educators led students through a planned curriculum and helped them to explore new knowledge. Before the current emphasis on testing, many learners felt excited about learning, and teachers felt free to accelerate or intervene individually in a student's learning cycle.

To guarantee continuous learning among all students, school districts must abandon their mindless reliance on state tests and No Child Left Behind legislation, and adopt a philosophy of mastery-level performance for all children.

Testing isolated bits of knowledge and enacting legislation that tinkers with a failed system will never improve schools. Excellent schools do not exist outside of each individual student who attends the school. Students and their parents, the people who employ students part-time and full-time, the people who teach and guide students know how they are doing.

For the most part, since 2000, in the United States, schools have reduced the curriculum to the expected content of their state's standardized test items. Students play the testing game, practice for the exams and report high levels of boredom with school. For genuine learning, many students turn to the Internet, My Space, Facebook, and Google. On the other hand, some students have teachers who engage their minds and spirits. They encounter many opportunities to explore the world of knowledge in a collegial discovery of how things seem to work. These students have teachers who show them how to unveil the underlying structures of language, math, science and the arts. Their school boards invest in the development of their teachers and administrators.

Effective school boards lead districts that achieve their mission. The members of these boards operate like outstanding governing boards in business and hospitals. Successful businesses respond to their customers; they delight their customers (Deming, 1994). School boards and senior executives who truly lead use effective feedback loops from members of the school community to guide their discussions, strategic planning, and assessment models.

Their feedback processes are well-planned and well-executed. They occur regularly, and preserve an historical record that often translates into trend data that reveal where a district is and where it has to go to achieve its mission.

In a study of the northeast of the United States, Burak (2006) found that effective districts had a clear sense of their role in curriculum evaluation and investment. Districts that make a difference for every child's learning cycle begin with curriculum design, implementation, and evaluation.

In other words, their superintendents and their school boards adopt the plan for curriculum development, implementation, and assessment. Adopting a viable curriculum is the only way to engage educators, parents, and community leaders in a dialogue that produces excellent schools (Marzano, 2003).

Inquiry is a basic skill that these school boards, their executives, and employees use to develop informed decisions that continuously improve the operations of the schools and student achievement.

To create effective schools in which all children learn, school boards, administrators, teachers, and parents must work together in the development of precise curriculum with a clear scope and sequence. They must adopt a monitoring process for implementation and assessment of the curriculum. They must critically analyze the actual results that the academic and cultural curricula of the schools produce. They must assess the culture of care at each school as well as academic achievement.

In the final analysis, full and complete curricula analysis leads to informed decisions. Policy boards and school leaders should make curricula decisions with educators and parents. The mission of the schools must be a community mission. Curricular design, feedback and assessment are the dynamic sources of energy that effective schools use to continuously improve instruction for students. Professional development and multiple assessments of student growth in cognitive and social-emotional development should guide the educational planning process in schools that work for students.

All students should be able to say: "I like my school. People are nice here. I am learning important things in my school."

Chapter 2

School District and Building Leadership

"Leaders are visionaries with a poorly developed sense of fear and no concept of the odds against them"

— Robert Jarvik

THE CURRENT REALITY FACING SCHOOL LEADERS

The pressure on schools and students to perform well on standardized tests has never been greater. The high-stakes testing environment endorsed and lauded by state and federal education departments forces many educators to choose between educating youth to live in the twenty-first century or prepare them to be successful on standardized, politically driven tests. According to Hargreaves and Fink (2006), "The constructive and compelling idea of standards—that learning comes before teaching and that we should be able to know and demonstrate when learning has occurred—has degenerated into a compulsive obsession with standardization (one literacy or mathematics program for everyone, one way to teach it, one size fits all) and a ruthless pursuit of market competition" (p. 6).

In 2000, the notion in the White House and in state houses throughout the United States seemed to be that pressure was the precedent to enhanced performance. Pressure-driven enterprises that utilize social normative stress and fear as motivators employ concepts that educators, physicians, and mental health specialists know to be false. Politicians and business leaders endorse pressure as part of free enterprise when it suits their needs.

25

Ironically, many educators and educational leaders initially gave tacit approval to this pressure-driven coercive management system. Those who did otherwise sparked the wrath of editorial boards and politicians who freely ridiculed them.

Simply put, the danger in today's high-stakes testing environment is that public educators will acquiesce and train their students to pass state exams, even if they know in their hearts that this is the wrong thing to do for the long-term benefit of the students.

In fact, Hargreaves and Fink (2006) suggest that the "education standards bubble" is about to burst in the United States, and that we need only look toward the United Kingdom, Australia, and many parts of Canada to see how these nations have already abandoned high-stakes testing as effective school reform. Not surprisingly, there is a great deal of research that suggests that organizations "almost universally change as little as they must, rather than as much as they should" (Hargreaves and Fink, 2006, p. 4).

Success for diverse students cannot be measured in a paper test like an emissions test that casts all cars into a one-size-fits-all solution. America's culture tends to endorse the quick fix which is particularly appealing to politicians, business leaders, and daily media pundits. School leaders and teachers who respond to these pressures for a quick solution to shocking failure rates among Hispanic males in high school are part of the larger problem that narrows curricula and motivates many students to leave school.

"No child left behind" has become a meaningless slogan that carries no more actual worth than "every child tested." At one time, no child left behind meant that public schools would do everything possible to provide sufficient time and appropriate opportunities and resources for each child to become a productive citizen. In 2009, the slogan means that all school children in grades three to twelve will sit for state-approved tests in English and math.

Educational leaders, school district leaders, and school leaders should reject the idea that effective schools drill and practice their students in test-taking skills until they have 90 percent of their students pass a standard test in English and math.

The educational standards of the fifty states and the tests that measure them should be viewed by all educators and parents as the lowest common denominator for cognitive processes. These tests fail to measure the skills, dispositions, and creative and critical thinking processes a productive nation needs in its youth. Why would we want our children to experience and master these low-level phenomena?

The best approach educators and parents can take towards the standards is to view them as the lowest expectations we can hold for our students, and ignore them. Educators and parents can educate children to high levels of mastery by varying program schedules and extending adult instruction for those who need special attention. Children who participate in effective tutorials within an extended school day improve how they learn, and gain knowledge that they can apply.

Successful schools have teachers who design curricula that engage the whole child, and they emphasize character education and service to others in curriculum and co-curriculum activities. We know that schools that engage students in the application of acquired knowledge, the exercise of judgment, and the development of confidence in their leadership skills work for students (Bloom, 1981; Wiggins and McTighe, 2005).

Deep learning among adults and students "is often also slow learning—critical, penetrative, thoughtful, and ruminative. It is learning that engages people's feelings and connects with their lives" (Hargreaves and Fink, 2006, p. 53).

If we are preparing our youth to pass state standard tests, we are not preparing our youth for citizenship in their community, nation or the world. Testing cannot build excellence into any social system (Deming, 1994).

Strong, moral leadership, a clear vision of how to prepare our high school graduates to be effective citizens in their community, and the inculcation of a spirit of inquiry among educators, parents, and students are the elements that produce a quality education. The testing charade that passes for education in the United States at the beginning of the 21st century is not education.

OPPORTUNITIES EMERGE FOR NEW EDUCATIONAL LEADERS

School leaders who are well educated, motivated, and highly skilled focus on teaching and learning. They balance leadership and managerial functions in an era punctuated "by rapidly evolving and changing conditions, severe time compression, and high degrees of ambiguity and uncertainty" (Salas, Cannon-Bowers, and Blickensderfer, 1997, p. 306). Bennis (1997) characterizes the present world scene as one of "contradictions, dilemmas and ambiguities" (p. 193). The contradictions and variability initiated by the intended and unintended consequences of high stakes testing under NCLB (2001) has led to further declines in graduation rates.

Even considering the best-case socioeconomic scenarios in middle-class communities, school performance changes constantly as populations shift and numerous students come to school unprepared to learn. Kanter, Stein and Jick (1992) pointed out that "organizations are never frozen, but are fluid entities with many 'personalities'" (p. 10).

Leaders and school board members are challenged to improve school outcomes in an environment of increasing expectations coupled with dwindling financial and social resources. States and local governments propose caps for property tax rates assigned to schools, add demands for higher achievement without any incentives, and offer no additional funds for schools. The normal middle-class child's school day of six hours, with 4.5 hours of academic instructional time, is not sufficient for poor children and children who come to school without the benefit of English as a first language.

Schools must insure that every child meets performance standards or children may be at risk of personal humiliation, of grade level retentions, and of failure to graduate high school. Under the laws governing NCLB, schools are now technically subject to closure, and school board members, faculty, and administrators may face removal if students fail to meet average yearly improvement targets. Under the No Child Left Behind legislation, all students must meet proficiency levels within the new standards by 2014.

The pace of the educational reform movement, combined with little specific guidance about how to achieve state and federal mandates, creates a decision-making climate overflowing with complexity and ambiguity. The needs-to-resource equation demonstrates that some districts cannot meet the challenges their constituents bring to school with the resources available to them. These districts are designed to produce failure. Dissolving the districts multiplies the failures.

The changing demographics of the 21st century American family present additional challenges for school leaders and communities. Leaders have to decide how to best meet the diverse needs of their community. They need flexibility to allocate the educational and financial resources necessary to achieve the mandated or desired results among students with diverse needs.

School leaders must be trained to grasp complexity and ambiguity, to work collaboratively, and to make decisions that are well-conceived, implemented, regularly evaluated, and refined to enact meaningful change (Senge et al., 2000). In this chapter, we outline the skills and abilities that leaders require to negotiate these turbulent, yet exciting times.

It is the role of leaders to overcome any and all obstacles they face, whether environmental, organizational, or political. It is the duty of leaders to ensure that the next generations of American students have the requisite skills, abilities, emotional intelligence, and the character necessary to live in today's ever-changing cultural and economic environment.

The tasks may be daunting, appear impossible and frighten some potential leaders. True leaders see challenges as an opportunity where they might excel. As John F. Kennedy told an audience in Indianapolis in 1959, "The Chinese use two brush strokes to write the word 'crisis.' One brush stroke stands for danger; the other for opportunity. In a crisis, be aware of the danger—but recognize the opportunity."

NEW LEADERSHIP FOR THE 21ST CENTURY

Effective leaders communicate well and continuously. They lead with vision, courage, conviction, purpose, a strong moral compass, and the ability to see the culture and context in which their organization lives. Effective leaders lead people, not concepts or slogans. As pointed out repeatedly by Gary Wills (1994) in his book, *Certain Trumpets*, leadership creates followers.

When we view schools as systems comprised of people in structured relationships, and examine the critical assets of the educational system, we come to find that aside from the physical assets of the school buildings themselves, our major asset center is people.

In schools, our faculty and staff are our most valuable resource, and in them—and parents—reside the leverages for system-wide change. The most potent leadership tools used by effective leaders are data analysis, inquiry, dialogue, reflection, and collaboration with diverse thinkers. Diverse people expand the productivity within a system (Page, Scott, 2008).

Effective leaders are always mindful of their organization's culture and the context in which it operates. Above all else, schools are social systems. According to Hoy and Miskel (2001), "As a social system, schools are characterized by an interdependence of parts, a clearly defined population, differentiation from its environment, a complex network of social relationships, and its own unique culture . . . the school as a social system calls attention to both the planned and unplanned—the formal and informal—aspects of organizational life" (p. 22).

Leaders, whether at the district or building level, must always be mindful of the internal and external forces placing demands upon their system.

Internally, the forces within a leader's organization that encourage sustainable change or inertia are the employees and the organizational culture. External politics, policies, fiscal realities, and community values affect an organization. Strong leaders, combined with willing and knowledgeable followers working in a collaborative and creative enterprise, can mitigate many of these forces and achieve laudable goals.

VISION MAKING

Effective leaders help all stakeholders to keep a laser-like eye on the core mission and vision of the school or the district. Within this context, leaders keep the "main thing the main thing" (Cottrell, 2002). In schools, our "main thing" is educating children. They are the reason that we, as educators and instructional support staff, exist at all. The "main thing" must be owned by the organization *and* its employees. It is widely acknowledged that organizations function best when all members of the organization understand and share the organization's culture, core mission and purpose (Rosenberger, 1997; Schein, 1985; Senge, 1990).

Therefore, it should be a central role and goal of leaders at every level to create common understanding and clarity (shared vision) around the organization's goals. Leaders must strive to create the capacity within every employee to align personal goals with the mission and vision of the organization.

In *The Fifth Discipline* (1990), and later in *Schools that Learn* (Senge et al., 2000), Senge and his colleagues point out that successful organizations create a shared vision in partnership with all stakeholders so that everyone understands and supports the vision.

In successful organizations all personnel achieve:

1. High levels of skill in their area of expertise (personal mastery),
2. Awareness of their own beliefs and assumptions (mental models) and how they influence their own thinking and the organization, as well as the ability to suspend their beliefs in order to acquire deeper understanding from others,
3. A common understanding of purpose and goals (shared vision),
4. The realization of how well, together, they learn as a team (team learning), and
5. The ability to integrate all of the aforementioned disciplines theoretically and practically (systems thinking) (Senge, et al., 2000, pp. 59–79).

The days when leaders led organizations by edict and an iron fist disappeared with the wired telephone as the preferred means of communication. In order for well-conceived change initiatives to be successful and sustainable, one person cannot be the sole vehicle for the vision, implementation, supervision, and evaluation of change initiatives.

From the perspective of sustainability, stereotypical, autocratic leadership never really worked long-term (Barnard, 1939). For most of the twentieth century, when the stakes were lower, competition and accountability were virtually nonexistent beyond America's borders, and life was far less complex, some leaders survived with an autocratic style. Unfortunately, the by-product of this management style was, at best, organizational compliance and short-lived gains. Today, innovation and immediate response to client needs are necessary for organizational survival, success, and sustainability.

Today, successful leaders build teams who lead, not teams who blindly follow the leader. Teams are diverse and are tasked with exploring important issues deeply so that they identify root causes of weaknesses. Interactive teams identify strengths that may be better deployed to take advantage of opportunities and address threats to future successes. These teams have the capacity to disagree without becoming disagreeable.

In organizations that maximize effectiveness, all constituents share expectations and intentions, and learn to work as a coherent group or team (Salas et al., 1997). Professional training and staff development for leaders and followers are requisites to increase the personal and professional capacity of the organization to achieve its goals and aspirations (Salas et al., 1997).

Aside from training and discipline, organizational effectiveness requires the leader to communicate clearly. Leaders must make a charge or team assignment and its decision-making authority clear, well-understood and constantly reinforced. All members of a planning team should be fluent with the organization's current reality. They should possess a common understanding and belief in the organization's vision. Team members should have the capacity to deeply engage in the process of inquiry and dialogue which, in turn, allows the collective wisdom of the team to emerge. It is collective wisdom and not common thinking that is the well from which all innovation springs.

A VIEW FROM 30,000 FEET

Today's effective school leaders see the big picture. They use a 360-degree view from an altitude of 30,000 feet. They see the spheres in which the school operates. Effective leaders gain this perspective through a systems view of the independent, codependent, and interdependent forces within the organization. They know the forces that attempt to impose their values and interests upon the organization. They prepare themselves and their relationships with external constituents so that they can manage such external forces as political, economic, natural occurrences, consumers, residents and parents.

James McGregor Burns (1978) described leadership as transformational when the leader avoided leading through bureaucratic policies and rules and instead constructed a community of followers who committed their energy and intelligence to a shared purpose.

In the 21st century, an effective leader creates a collaboratively designed vision for the organization, builds the capacity of the organization to fulfill the mission, and then formulates a collaborative team to execute the plan.

McGregor Burns (1978) believed that transformational leaders would build a synergy between leaders and followers that guided the entire organization to "higher levels of morality and achievement" (p. 20). In 1990, Senge motivated many executives to adopt a systems approach in leading their organizations. He recommended that the elements that comprised an enterprise be viewed as interdependent social systems that produced multiple effects beyond the sum of their parts.

Within the arena of education, Leithwood, Jantzi, and Steinback (1999) argued that transformational leadership had the potential to move schools beyond surface-level changes to interpersonal structural changes in policies and practices that deeply altered the culture of schools and empowered a synergetic teaching and learning process.

Hargreaves and Fink (2006) offer a continuum of distributed leadership that has as its ultimate goal "Assertive Distribution" wherein leaders of organizations are:

> steadfast and passionate about shared purposes and values. Stimulate wide-ranging debate about important proposals. Involve resisters early. Include and listen to minorities. Use processes that surface thoughtful divergence and disagreement. Demonstrate the value of learning from differences. Be prepared for criticism but insist on respectful dialogue. Keep your sense of humor. Ensure that the vigorous professional culture always moves you forward. Never abrogate responsibility. Always reaffirm your goals. (p. 138)

Ironically, typical training programs for leaders often focus on improving the content knowledge of the individual for discrete aspects of their work such as finance, literacy, mathematics, supervision, community relations, and political skills. Little attention is paid to increasing the capacity of future leaders to learn and reflect on new learning, and to generate new knowledge collectively and collaboratively with a team.

New leaders rarely learn how to use systems thinking and systems tools to analyze the organization deeply, and to make decisions that are both culturally sensitive and inclusive as well as technically sound for schools and school children.

Staff development for school leaders should focus on systems thinking, creative problem solving, research-based learning, and diverse and collaborative inquiry. School leaders must master the facilitation of dialogue with instructional and instructional support staff, parents, and students, employers, and college admission officers.

COLLABORATION AND COLLEGIALITY

Schools today are incredibly complex. The domains in which school leaders must lead and manage extend across numerous distinct, yet interrelated systems: curriculum, pedagogy, student management and support, finance, facilities, transportation, cafeteria and food services, construction and bonds, debt management, insurance and risk management, personnel development, hiring, supervision, and the evaluation and termination of staff.

School leaders work with academic and social/emotional literacy initiatives. They evaluate faculty and staff, balance the needs of the general education and the special education population and their advocacy groups, and cope with numerous unfunded mandates, ever-changing rules and court decisions.

They manage diverse employee groups, work with school boards, and handle the day-to-day tasks of the budget, transportation programs, plant and facilities that challenge the skills, stamina and values of most school executives.

For example, management of the school lunch program presents many cultural and physical challenges. Often, the best decisions for children and education conflict with politics, resources, and community culture. School leaders have to dedicate sufficient time to examine and resolve conflicts about lunch programs concerns before addressing educational issues. Every action of the school is open to criticism. School leaders must build a partnership with the parents and staff. They have to earn their trust and support. Sustainable partnerships require a school leader with a clear vision and the patience to expend sufficient time with parents and staff to gain their understanding and commitment to the mission.

Candidates for the superintendent's position must consider some very practical questions such as: If test scores are low, do we shift our emphasis toward test prep? At what expense to the district budget and to student engagement in new learning do we pursue more test preparation activities?

Sometimes, the pressure to perform well on standardized assessments and the accompanying test prep become the educational program, and other cultural and developmental processes for children are abandoned to favor student success on state exams.

Superintendents have to exercise moral leadership. Their values and virtues must be fully developed to guide a district through the natural storms that life presents.

What is the right way to go? Take the case of new information influencing teaching and learning. Over the last ten years, the knowledge we have gained about how the brain works and how learning occurs has opened new vistas for educational practice. Yet, on a practical level, much of this new information has not reached the classroom. Little research-based information about how the brain learns has influenced pedagogical practices. Today, testing is what drives instruction, not a vision of how children learn.

Given the speed at which new information becomes available, it is impossible for a leader to make good decisions in all domains based upon what he or she knows individually. One may be an expert in managing a building, and yet have little knowledge about how to lead a change initiative.

A principal may be terrific at handling kids in disciplinary situations while having few ideas about pedagogy in Math or Science. Of course, the ideal situation is to have someone who excels in every domain, however unlikely that may be. To be effective, school leaders must learn how to delegate and share leadership with their instructional and instructional support staff.

DIFFERENT SKILLS FOR A DIFFERENT CENTURY

School district leaders in the 21st century require different skills than school leaders of the past. The content knowledge that the new leader needs is to understand systems and organizational behavior. To mobilize the latent wisdom and talent in an organization so that all stakeholders support learning and personal growth, superintendents must understand how to motivate and reward educators for leading learning innovations.

In essence, the new leader must have the theories, methods and tools to create a "Learning Community" (Senge, 1990). Senge advocates that one of the core disciplines of a learning organization is *team learning;* it is an essential discipline for school leaders that can and should be practiced by the entire organization. *Team learning* is "a discipline of practices designed, over time, to get people of a team thinking and acting together" (Senge et al., 2000, p. 73).

Team learning is based on the concept of alignment, which connotes the arrangement of a group of scattered elements so they function as a whole. In other words, to borrow a metaphor from Crew, all oars are rowing with the same stroke at the same time and in the same direction. The ultimate goal is to elegantly develop efficiency and effectiveness among all the rowers to win the race.

In the presence of *team learning,* organizational efforts move in a common direction, with people understanding and supporting one another. They display the ability to truly understand and respect each other. Team learners yearn to understand before they try to be understood and accepted.

Organizationally, leaders first develop *team learning* in their schools through inquiry and dialogue which is designed to create a common awareness within their organization about the current reality. The leader uses the organization's current reality to form the basis of a collectively generated, shared vision of the future.

Alignment is not about creating a one-size-fits-all methodology of reaching organizational goals. "When team members become familiar with each others' knowledge, skills, abilities, motivations, preferences, and style, they are able to better anticipate teammates' task, informational, and interpersonal needs" (Salas et al., 1997, p. 307).

The discipline of *team learning,* when practiced faithfully, helps to galvanize a school district or building personnel around the core purpose of the organization. *Team learning* increases understanding and commitment among all students and adults within a healthy socioemotional context. This, in turn, ripens the organizational culture for successful, sustainable change.

BUILDING POWERFUL RELATIONSHIPS

Few leaders can interest their followers to become more collaborative if their relationship with faculty and staff is not built on a foundation of mutual trust and respect. The three R's of leadership are as follows: Relationships, Relationships, and Relationships. In school systems that work for students, leaders develop strong professional relationships with all constituent groups.

Sergiovanni (1994) speaks about the concepts of bridging *and* bonding as essential for the health of any organization. Most organizations, certainly schools, have compartmentalized components. In *Central Office,* multiple centralized functions comprise the divisions of administrative roles such as the Superintendent's Office, Instruction, Pupil Personnel Services, Human Resources, Business, Building, and Grounds and Food Services.

Schools typically have departments, grade levels, special areas, and other separate and distinct services that create barriers between people within and without the organization. Generally, it is good and necessary for those workers within a department to form a professional "bond" with each other. Problems occur when the bonding is so strong or weak that it detracts from the mission of the school.

Well-bonded groups that fail to bridge with each other and that do not establish mutual missions and goals detract from the success of the larger enterprise. They fulfill their own self-interests at the expense of the larger mission. Healthy organizations establish patterns for both bonding and bridging to occur among all divisions. They achieve a balance among staff and school interests through a shared vision which is the key to a cohesive school.

Consider the example of a professional orchestra. Ideally, each section of the orchestra rehearses independently of the full orchestra. Over time, each section builds its capacity to play together. The members bond into a strong unit. When the time comes for all sections to come together, the talent of each section is used to bridge their independent strengths and form an intra-dependent and co-dependent, holistic performance.

An orchestra creates a synergy that makes the collective performance more powerful than the sum of its parts. When the orchestra works as one creative system, the result is a magnificent performance that transports the audience and the musicians to a magical place of harmony and emotional stimulation.

Of course, this amalgamation does not happen on its own. The leader of the orchestra is the conductor and it is her or his task to get the most out of every individual player and section. Each section must capture and relay to the audience the essence of the musical composition. If the conductor is highly respected, the orchestra is more likely to develop a trust and willingness to follow his or her lead. If not—well, suffice it to say—the best orchestras do not come together under a less-than-able leader.

The successful conductor, like any leader, must exhibit personal mastery with the music. The performance is highly dependent on her ability to communicate her vision of the music to the orchestra and then by design, through collective experimentation and practice develop a means to bring her vision to fruition in how the orchestra executes a performance. The successful conductor "bridges" the talent of each section and blends sectional uniqueness into a magnificent performance.

It is notable also that the audience at a concert, truly the major constituency, is more likely to enjoy the performance when it senses that the conductor and the orchestra are playing with one bow. It is this intangible sense of harmony and design, this fluid and creative invention, that is often discernable and at the same time hard to describe, that separates great from good performances.

Of course, our orchestral analogy describes the outcome of a strong, trusting, respectful relationship between the conductor, lead chairs, performers and audience that often has to be built over time.

School leadership has many similarities and parallels that can be compared to the orchestral analogy. For a school to perform exceptionally well, every department must be made up of talented teachers. Diverse faculty must develop the ability to work together as a unit to make an entire department strong. Like an orchestra, the school succeeds synergistically when all departments come together and join with a leader who has the ability to communicate and teach a vision. Constituents and educators who work together in a focused manner to produce a shared vision for their students achieve the desired outcomes.

When we view a successful leader, we usually see the by-product of his or her effectiveness in the behavior of the people the leader trained and developed. What we rarely see, and what needs to be discussed, is how these outcomes are achieved through the development of trusting and credible relationships that reflect high moral values, ethical practices, personal integrity, and responsibility.

INQUIRY: AN ESSENTIAL SKILL FOR BUILDING RELATIONSHIPS AND SHARED VISION

Most leaders that are new to a role experience a honeymoon period. The actual length of the honeymoon depends largely on the leader's behavior, his or her cultural awareness, a capacity to build strong, healthy professional relationships, and personal integrity.

How often have we seen new leaders, without a deep understanding of the social system of the district or school, enter into a new position with an agenda for change and fail within a year? Too often new leaders and their agenda fail within their first six months on the job. Sometimes the agenda for change belongs to the new leader; sometimes it belongs to a school board. Occasionally, change is transported in from another social system. In every case, change enacted too soon is a recipe for disaster.

Unfortunately, there is often no recovery from a bad or an ill-conceived, poorly designed start. The issue a new leader faces is how to introduce change in ways that employees will perceive as worthwhile. Employees want to know how and with whom change initiatives are formed, and who will benefit and who might be harmed from the changes.

How do effective leaders initiate and manage effective change endeavors, and maintain respectful and healthy relationships with stakeholders and constituents? Let's first discuss our definition of a strong, healthy professional relationship.

Leaders must accept that "being liked" professionally is a by-product of "being respected." Respect is not given or earned overnight. Leaders gain respect by conveying clear goals, determination and enough concern for other people that followers know they will have the leaders' support.

If a leader's primary goal is to be "liked," change will be next to impossible to achieve. Ironically, faculties and staffs rarely stay "in like" with a leader if the district or building is poorly managed. When inconsistency is the only consistency, or avoidance is the major leadership tactic employed to "resolve" issues, followers disappear.

A strong, healthy professional relationship between staff and school leaders is based on credibility, trust, and respect. Often, these traits are in conflict with the "like quotient." Credibility, trust and respect are earned through a consistent vision and the practice of substantive values and virtues. Being liked should not be as important to a leader as being judged fair and competent.

Typically, the staff disposition that reflects a "like" for a school leader is a healthy by-product of trust and respect based upon the time and effort that the leader expended to build a relationship with the staff and to develop a shared vision.

An important skill that all leaders must master is the skill of actively listening to one's self as well as to others. This is done by asking many questions that illuminate the patterns of behavior that a leader observes. Such questions are designed to get as much data as possible from as many people as possible. Only with multiple lines of feedback can the leader accurately interpret the events she or he observes.

The questions leaders ask should be framed as queries, not accusations. Most should start with a simple phrase like, "I'm wondering . . ." For instance:

1. "I've been observing bus arrivals for the past three weeks. I'm wondering why we handle bus arrivals in this manner. Has anyone ever gotten hurt?" Or, "I wonder if there is a better way we could handle this that wouldn't place an unfair burden on any one individual or group of teachers, a better way to ensure the safety of our children, and get everyone to class in a safe, calm, and timely way?"

2. "I'm wondering why our procurement process takes so many days. Have there ever been any complaints from the school board, parents, or employees that teachers and students do not have the supplies they need? Is there a way we could maintain fiscal integrity and speed up the process to better ensure educational success?"

3. "Hi, Mrs. Smith, I hate to disturb your prep period, however, I just had a call from Mrs. Jones and she was very upset about her child's academic progress. I'm wondering if you have any insights into her concerns that you could share with me."

4. "I have spent a great deal of time reviewing our student performance data with our school improvement team, and consequently have noticed certain patterns emerge. Some patterns are quite positive and others are less so. My purpose is to make you aware of these patterns and enlist your help in identifying the factors that contribute to these results."

Clearly, questions are important factors. Equally, if not more important, is the need for the leader to listen deeply to the answers to these questions and the inspirations they reveal. Effective leaders follow each answer with more questions that produce even deeper understandings about the "whys" behind an event or pattern of events.

When the leader responds to an answer with a judgmental statement like, "Well, that's just silly," or worse, the leader's response causes a shutdown or a confrontation, it prevents the leader from achieving the overall goal of building strong, healthy professional relationships.

A leader can avoid unnecessary confrontations by being circumspect and sensitive about the frame of a question or a comment. In the example presented here, when the leader is judgmental and critical of ideas, she or he causes distrust, and runs the risk of creating additional problems, not solving existing ones.

Over time, patterns of verbal and physical behavior actually define the attitudes, beliefs, and assumptions or culture of the organization. The leader needs to be aware of how s/he is contributing to the culture of the school. Through proper inquiry, leaders expose information and mine the knowledge and wisdom of the staff. Wisdom that personnel share with a leader helps to transform a system, school district, and a school into a highly professional enterprise.

The goal is to achieve a shared vision, no matter how much it may conflict with a leader's prior knowledge and assumptions about how things should work. Effective leaders ask additional questions and pursue informational paths that reveal a deeper understanding about why the system behaves as it does. The need for system change is part of the shared vision and must be discovered by the stakeholders.

The use of inquiry as a primary leadership strategy is essential to get other people to expose their attitudes, beliefs, and assumptions about an issue, problem, or cultural perspective. Inquiry provides the leader with more and better data about the underlying mental models and structures that are literally causing a problem or presenting a barrier to change.

ROOT-CAUSE ANALYSIS

Better data from a wide range of sources allow for greater perspective about an issue. Root-cause analysis and change require accurate data from diverse sources. Better data within a cultural context lead to better decisions. Better decisions communicated clearly to stakeholders build common understanding. Common understanding elicits buy-in, and buy-in leads to gaining support. Supporters open systems to synergy; and synergy leads to respectful, trusting, professional relationships that achieve transformational change.

Transformational leadership is possible when relationships are right and the mission is clear and shared by all stakeholders. The more familiar a leader is with the culture of the organization, the more likely cultural transformation can occur. Inquiry is a means to help a leader unearth artifacts that reveal the culture and its strengths, weaknesses, opportunities and threats. These artifacts may be intangible.

Often, the most important feedback to a leader comes with intangibles like attitudes, beliefs, and assumptions (mental models) that govern the way people within a culture behave. School leaders cannot lead without understanding the culture of the schools and communities they serve.

Leadership through inquiry also helps the leader avoid "push-back." A system truism is that all imposed structures produce push-back. This is a phenomenon that occurs when the leader identifies a problem and issues a directive or imposes a structural fix without taking the time to investigate causality, sufficiently identify and design for the intended and unintended consequences of the change, or communicate all of the above effectively to affected constituents.

Clearly, to reduce push-back from constituents and employees, leaders must share ownership. Constituent "buy-in" must include a shared sense of commitment and responsibility among all stakeholders. At best, directives create compliance. Usually, they create minimal compliance and subtle attempts to make someone else's solution fail.

Push-back commonly occurs because an edict is given and compliance is expected. No one knows why the decision was necessary in the first place. Frequently, such decisions were communicated through informal channels. The biggest problem for the leader occurs when the faculty and staff begin to "wonder" about the leader's capacity to lead.

Take the scenario with Mrs. Smith (item 3) on page 38 and shift some "facts." Let's assume for the moment that you as a leader have some concerns about Mrs. Smith and the way she handles children and parents. If you as a leader start the conversation with, "Hi, Mrs. Smith, I just had a call from Mrs. Jones and she was very upset about her child's academic progress. This is the second call this week. Now, what happened this time?" you will experience push-back first hand.

More importantly, you will close the door on learning more about Mrs. Smith and gaining insight into both her behavior and the problem with Mrs. Jones's child. Furthermore, when Mrs. Smith goes to the faculty room or to her union delegate, imagine the comments that will be made about you. While you may not care what she says, over time those types of conversations build up "grey stamps" that the faculty will "cash in" when they have had enough of you and your leadership (Senge, Roberts, Kleiner, Ross, and Smith, 1999).

If you truly have an issue with Mrs. Smith's handling of children and parental complaints, a different discussion is more fruitful. It might go something like this:

Hi, Mrs. Smith, I just had a call from Mrs. Jones and she was very upset about her child's academic progress. You know, I have received two calls this week with similar parent complaints. I am concerned for you and that you are okay. I'm wondering if you could shed some light on the parental issues with these specific children. Also, can you give me some insight into how we can resolve these issues?

This approach doesn't necessarily guarantee that there won't be push-back from a teacher who is adversely affected by change initiatives. Sometimes, the response from an individual or group affected by a change initiative carries elements of true insight that need to be considered. Opposition should be viewed as opportunity to rethink and more carefully analyze a change initiative. Opposition is not a barrier to success. Often, mean-spirited or well-intentioned opposition carry kernels of truth that need examination.

If someone presents an emotionally charged response, a leader's best response is to assess what the respondent has been experiencing and to exercise concern and use inquiry. When complaint patterns like this emerge suddenly, something has changed recently in one party's life. The changing patterns are merely symptoms of deeper issues that will require time and inquiry to discover root causes.

When a leader stays in inquiry, the means to assess the "root cause" issues and to formulate a plan that properly responds to the issue emerge in a way that makes everyone successful.

The goal of a leader should be to build the capacity to see one's school or school system clearly, and to build respectful, collegial relationships with all stakeholders. Stewardship is the art of building relationships and expressing a caring concern for and an investment in the success of others. It is a fundamental disposition for effective leaders.

The key to building these positive and consistently authentic relationships is how the leader uses the tool of inquiry. Teaching faculty and staff how to use inquiry effectively—in the classroom, in the office, in teaching, and in discipline—helps all stakeholders to mature into a stronger community of learners.

Once everyone leads with inquiry, relationships deepen and a commitment to the school and its mission becomes possible.

CREATING GUIDING IDEAS: THE KEYS TO CONSISTENCY AND PURPOSE

Once leaders have followers, the question becomes, "Where are we going?" At first glance, stating a mission and purpose would seem to be a simple task. Yet, leaders often forget the power of guiding ideas that explicitly express the attitudes, beliefs, and assumptions of systemic expectations. In other words, the context in which one leads, teachers teach, students learn, and parents support learning is as important as the clarity of the mission statement.

By explicitly stating one's personal beliefs and promoting an explicit statement of a school's collective beliefs in the form of guiding ideas, everyone working in or associated with the school or district is able to understand what is expected of them.

Consistently-applied and wisely-chosen guiding ideas express cultural norms and support the structure from which shared vision, collective wisdom, and common understanding launch. Guiding ideas form the basis for substantive, sustainable change.

Guiding ideas are typically somewhat ambiguous, general, and appealing statements (Stone 1996). Because of their ambiguity and paradoxical clarity, it is relatively easy to get people to agree with them conceptually. For instance, "No Child Left Behind" or "All children can learn" or "All children and adults in this school will be treated with dignity and respect at all times" are all examples of guiding ideas. Even though most educators have serious concerns about the implementations of the NCLB legislation, most agree that we should never leave any child behind.

In fact, educators' responses to NCLB represent a classic example of "push-back" by stakeholders who did not share in the design, development, and implementation efforts to construct a national policy.

NCLB, as federal policy, represents a set of structures that are largely politically driven. Its principles were imposed upon the field of education with little input, discussion, or resources. The reaction is entirely predictable, and, unfortunately, the guiding idea, as admirable and inspirational as it could be, gets mired in the underlying lack of respect for educators.

Many teachers feel that the crafters of NCLB have no idea of the challenges that teachers face with poor populations in schools that have not been assigned the resources children need to acquire a sound education.

In fact, some educators now believe that we actually should leave some students behind in order to motivate them to take personal responsibility for their education. Others believe, as we do, that students should face school exit exams that reflect national criteria like the core ACT exams. We believe that permanent and universal national standards would help all parents, students, teachers, administrators and community leaders know where youth in their community stand academically. Such exams might indicate how much additional help the schools will need for their students to achieve high performance on these criterion-referenced tests.

The struggle in America's schools is more accurately described as the challenge to have all children achieve mastery-level performance. Proficiency is inadequate in a global economy. If China and India achieve mastery levels of educational achievement for ten percent of their twelfth graders, collectively they will have two students at mastery level for every twelfth grader in the United States.

RAISE THE BAR BEYOND NO CHILD LEFT BEHIND

Effective leaders focus on what schools can do without federal and state interventions. No Child Left Behind is the classic case of how not to institute change. It is clearly coercive and punitive in its applications and punishments applied to school leaders and their staff. No wonder that cheating and fraud have increased in schools. No wonder that passive resistance, student dropout rates, and teacher departures from the profession have increased.

These kinds of central government missteps are the actions that prompted our founding fathers to do whatever they could to protect local control of schools against central governments and their historical tyrannies.

However, as frustrating as it is, NCLB is the law of the land. As a leader, one can not let the discontent with NCLB fester within one's school culture. If festering resentment and cynicism is allowed to spread, in no time at all, faculty and staff can become totally demoralized or even rebelliously destructive. It is up to the leader to prevent this from happening.

Guiding ideas help to focus the leader's community around a mission that everyone can support. The goal is to reframe the issue or problem and capture positive energy that propels the school or school district toward its vision of success without becoming mired in deficit thinking (Carter, 2001).

Effective school leaders focus all constituents on the strengths they have individually and collectively. They set high and far-reaching goals that depend on the will of the stakeholders in the school and offer a clear mission and vision of the future. They also present ways to collaborate and build a new structure and system to meet the new vision. They inspire the staff to work together and the school to change.

We recommend that every school system with eighth graders and twelfth graders adopt the ACT Exams in math, science, social studies and English as their exiting exams. Do not wait for federal and state action. Lead. Get others to follow. Push students to mastery levels and promote Advanced Placement exams for students as well as county civil service and professional licensing and union exams.

Districts should assign some of their revenue to pay for the administration of these exams to their students. Foundations can be established in local communities, large and small cities to raise non-tax dollars that will support these opportunities for students to demonstrate their knowledge in a fair playing field.

The testing issues associated with NCLB would dissipate as schools took responsibility for their own accountability. Part of moving beyond the bureaucratic limits of NCLB is to frame questions that guide schools to achieve grander missions than student scores on an exam.

Let's reframe some of the questions associated with NCLB. School leaders could ask: "How could we design and implement NCLB in a way that actually produced evidence that no child was being left behind?" Accompanying questions, in no particular order, might be:

1. What would it look and feel like in our school or district if the guiding idea of No Child Left Behind meant no child would be without the mastery skills required of a productive citizen in our society, and what if this was the actual mission of the schools? How would we execute that mission and how would we know we had done a good job?
2. What practices that we presently employ in the classroom or school would need to be either abandoned or modified to enable NCLB's guiding idea to become a living and breathing mission of every school in our district?
3. What more do we need to learn and be able to do to allow NCLB's guiding idea to be a mission that we execute daily?
4. What funding resources can we reallocate to make NCLB's guiding idea come alive?
5. What teaching resources can we reallocate to make NCLB's guiding idea come alive?
6. What additional staff resources can we reallocate to make NCLB's guiding idea come alive?
7. What can we do to educate parents and business leaders so that they will become valuable partners with our schools and enable NCLB's guiding idea to come alive?

Questions like, "How can we avoid dealing with NCLB?" are not productive and probably unethical, if not illegal. The educational leader's role is to lead the inquiries, to promote speculation about how the community can do more for our students, and how to motivate our students to do more for themselves.

Within the context of the realities facing the school or school district, educational leaders need to encourage teachers to commit to a more profound mission, a more necessary dream for our youth and our country. Every one of those questions outlined above might become a guiding idea for a school or district.

We like to think of the question pathway indicated previously as a set of those Russian Nesting Dolls. Within each large doll lie many smaller dolls. If we think of "No Child Left Behind" as representing the guiding idea for the largest doll, what could the next guiding idea be? Often the generation of new ideas and actions begin with an "if/then" statement such as, "If we believe no child should be left behind, then . . ."

The answers to our questions mirror the attitudes, beliefs, and assumptions of one's culture and community. Each idea would have intended benefits and consequences, innovations and theories, methods, and tools required to implement them. There would not be right or wrong ideas as long as one stays within the boundaries of ethical decisions, equity of opportunity, fairness, and concern for each child to do well.

Some ideas will be better than others. The execution of guiding ideas reveals their value. The goal is to find the highest leveraging strategy possible: the one that produces the most results for the greatest number, and the one that continues to consider those who have been left out.

The guiding ideas should reflect the best thinking of a collective group of constituents who collaborate and get "buy-in" from almost all stakeholders. This process of "drilling down" ultimately exposes high-leverage opportunities and root-cause solutions.

Some questions that leaders could pose to their constituents would be:

1. "No Child Left Behind!" If we believe that no child should be left behind, then . . .
   Every child must be taught to read, write, speak, and listen at proficient levels (Design for mastery levels and celebrate proficiency).
2. If we believe that every child must be taught to read, write, speak, and listen at proficient levels, then . . .
   Every teacher must possess the capacity to diagnose and prescribe reading interventions using a highly differentiated instructional model.
3. If we believe that every teacher must possess the capacity to diagnose and prescribe reading interventions using a highly differentiated instructional model, then . . .
   Every teacher must receive targeted professional development in the diagnosis and interventions necessary to have students comprehend the texts they read in all subjects.

Creating guiding ideas is just the beginning of the change process. Yet, it is an absolutely critical step in creating buy-in for any change initiative. Not only is buy-in important, the common understandings and relationships built during this process are the fuel required to sustain initiative. In the early stages of change, where things are bound to go wrong and the initial excitement over the initiative wanes, common understandings and relationships sustain change.

Michael Fullan (2001) speaks to this issue when he describes the "Implementation Dip." He notes that leaders must anticipate a dip in enthusiasm among staff as the implementation of a change initiative takes root and obstacles and difficulties are discovered. Leaders must plan to celebrate small successes, state doable objectives, and guide the momentum to change.

INNOVATION AND CHANGE

An innovation or new initiative begins with the leader conducting deep, truthful conversations with people within and adjacent to the organization about its current state. Results that the school produces would be examined and growth opportunities would be identified. Vision defines future opportunities and motivates people to change. Change is a long, sometimes tedious, yet vitally necessary process.

HOW DATA INFORM CHANGE

The first step in any change initiative is to have a clear picture of one's current reality that includes a thorough, data-driven review of performance results in all pertinent domains. The goal of any data collection effort should be to establish as accurate and detailed a picture of one's current institutional performance and culture as possible.

Use data—not opinions, guesses, and impressions. The analysis of data can be a painful process. The leader has to assure everyone that the goal is not to find fault or assess blame. Leaders convince followers that an honest assessment of current strengths, weaknesses, opportunities, and threats within and outside the school system requires new goals.

Change leaders must make sure no one *is* blamed for the findings that emerge. If the leader fails to follow through on this promise, and fails to create a safe space for all participants, then often this omission brings an end to the change initiative for years to come.

What leaders and stakeholders need to know is that a school or school district produces the outcomes it was *designed to produce*. Digest that for a moment. A system produces the results it was designed to produce (Deming, 1994).

In fact, all systems have design, and all workers function within or in opposition to the design of the system to which they are assigned. It can be no other way. If, over time, a pattern is observed that 40 percent of your students are scoring at levels 1 and 2 on state assessments, it is because your system is designed to consistently produce those results. Hard to believe, you say? Sorry, think it through. It's painfully accurate.

The only way to change the pattern of results produced by systemic design is to create a new vision about the desired future (Senge, 1990). Senge suggests that four principles should guide a change effort: (1) Establish guiding ideas—specific evidence that would prove that the guiding idea was realized should be identified at the outset, (2) create innovative infrastructures designed to produce valued results, (3) teach those charged with producing the evidence of success the theories, methods and tools necessary to be successful, and (4) measure progress deeply and regularly, and guide reflective dialogue with representative constituents to keep the initiative alive and continuously refined.

If the system of instruction at your school or school system was capable of performing better, it would be producing a different result. No matter how hard a leader tries, cajoles, or rewards changed behaviors, the system will revert to its prior performance levels unless relationships, beliefs, and shared goals change.

Most of what administrators typically do to initiate change is to tinker around the edges of what the system design requires. Tinkering does not improve systems or achieve better results. It will never work—at least not for very long. Whatever bounce in results tinkering achieves, it will be temporary at best.

Frequently, those involved with adjusting a bad system soon abandon the process and report yet another failed change initiative. They revert to previously-learned behaviors and return to blaming the leader, the students, the parents, and even each other.

No wonder almost 40 percent of new teachers become cynical, leave within the first five years of their teaching career, and suffer a variety of stress-related illnesses.

Leaders who know systems theory, who examine their own and others' mental models, who develop a shared vision, who understand how teams learn and how to motivate themselves and others break the cycle of failure in their schools, and rally staff around a change initiative.

They build consensus on the innovations necessary to achieve desired results. They express authentic concern for others and they model integrity and personal responsibility. They create schools that work for all students and for the communities with responsive and flexible systems.

Chapter 3

Diagnostics, Prescriptions, and Assessments for Success

School systems that work for all children develop learning communities wherein all stakeholders share a common understanding of what the vision, mission, and goals of the school system are. Learning communities focus on student learning and continuous growth. Teaching skills align to curricula designs. Professional development, hiring, and evaluation practices support the mission, vision, and goals of the school district.

Effective school systems use data to inform every decision. They are obsessed with measurement. They are not obsessed with standardized test scores. They seek to design a mosaic of data sources that reveal how well the system is doing in pursuit of its vision, mission, and goals.

Effective systems share a passion for creating data systems that deliver information to teachers in a timely way. They use data to differentiate and customize instruction for maximum student growth. The frequency of measurement, its form, and the availability of the data enable faculty, parents, and even students to know how to continuously improve.

The data collected illuminates what the system values academically, socially, emotionally, physically, and artistically for every child.

Many educational communities make valiant attempts to be data-informed. Unfortunately, the data that many school systems rely upon to inform curriculum development and instructional strategies reflect individual performance on group tests. Such data are not helpful from the perspective of creating a school system that works for all children.

Since the advent of NCLB, many districts focus their data analysis on standardized state tests or other similar measures. At best, these tests identify who learned what they were supposed to learn within a prescribed time period. The data provided by these tests are often summative, not formative, and have little value in improving the teaching and learning process. What is particularly frightening is how dependent many districts have become on data from these tests to guide instruction, curriculum, and programs.

Doug Reeves (2000) once compared a formative test to a physical examination, and a summative test to an autopsy. While the autopsy might provide information about the end of a patient's life, it does little to prevent the patient from dying.

Schools systems that succeed with all children use multiple sources of data to ensure that their students thrive. Failing is not an option. School systems should examine the quality of the data they collect, not the quantity. The data should inform teachers and administrators about student progress toward meeting school and system goals.

Perhaps most importantly, data must provide frequent feedback about individual student progress. Data should offer information that teachers can use to differentiate or modify instruction. Data should be diagnostic, and the subsequent prescriptions they suggest must be customized to the specific needs of each learner.

In school systems that work for all children, data collection methods are also designed and analyzed to determine how well the entire school system is moving toward achieving its stated vision, mission, and goals. Data are gathered frequently and used for both formative and summative purposes, and all stakeholders have access to the data. Summative data are shared with site-based teams to identify large-scale gaps in student comprehension of math and literacy requirements. Individual student data in multiple assessments provide pictures of each student's progress.

When data do not confirm that progress towards stated goals has occurred, the organization quickly recognizes the dissonance. Stakeholder reaction is quick and widespread because the selected procedure or teaching strategy is not producing mastery for all students. Systemic adjustments are made efficiently. Nothing gets too far out of alignment, and the system stays on course to help each child make progress.

In successful school systems, all stakeholders share ownership in the system's vision, mission, and goals. Everyone is empowered within responsive school systems to note a gap between results and expectations. The system serves none more than the students and the community it represents.

The purpose of this chapter is to give leaders the ability to clearly see their operational systems. We hope to provide school leaders with tools that consistently distinguish effective school systems from those that are ineffective. We hope to guide leaders and their leadership teams to organize and use data in ways that serve the needs of students.

DIAGNOSIS
Data, Data Everywhere

Contrary to some public perceptions, teachers, administrators, and school *intro* improvement teams frequently pour over reams of data that are generated by an agency other than their own. The problem that teachers encounter is that too much student data are available and too little are useful. Most of the data schools receive support state efforts to measure student progress towards state and federal standards. Data quantity far exceeds data quality.

Nationwide, school systems are trying desperately to use the data standardized tests provide to diagnose learning issues and prescribe changes to instructional practices and curriculum so that their students meet the state standards. Unfortunately, despite good intentions, in many cases systemic progress is limited.

Recent reports indicate that the number of schools nationwide that failed to meet AYP has risen 28 percent between the 2007–08 and 2006–07 school years (Hoff, 2009). Even where systems are meeting standards, success is largely defined by the quantity of students approaching or meeting proficiency—not mastery performance. Proficiency is a standard which will hasten our students' inability to compete on the world stage.

We have never met any school board trustees, leaders, faculty, or staff who wanted their students to fail. Yet, students continue to fail in significant numbers, particularly in systems with high needs and low resources. One reason for student failure is that school systems are so focused on being compliant with a variety of requirements set for them by state education systems that they have lost their primary goal: to educate each child.

There is so much emphasis on compliance with Adequate Yearly Progress (AYP) standards, test scores, and graduation rates that many districts have actually created compliance structures with new administrative roles strictly focused on minimum requirements for success.

Compliance is not a bad thing; in fact, the law requires it. However, there is no law that mandates that compliance be your systemic focus or mission. There is no law that states you cannot design a system that far exceeds mandates. In compliant systems, test preparation of students is the only curriculum.

Frankly, efforts to comply distract districts from focusing on teaching and learning. Greatness is rarely achieved by being compliant. Successful school systems comply with all mandates placed upon them; however, they are not preoccupied by them. Their compliance is a byproduct of their focus on the teaching and learning process.

Many school systems rely too heavily on data associated with standardized test performance. Data produced by a state's education department typically report compliance with NCLB and state mandates. Such data reveal who achieved proficiency on what they were supposed to learn by the requisite deadline. Some data reveal the number of students meeting certain indicators or dispositions within a given standard. Over time, certain patterns might emerge that could reveal gaps in the curriculum or weaknesses in instructional practice. In this sense, standardized data can be helpful to school leaders and teachers.

Too late However, the data that standardized tests provide rarely help teachers in their quest to improve a particular child's learning, in part because data reports rarely reach teachers in a timely manner. The information they contain often pertains to children who are no longer their students. Individual data do not reveal a child's thinking and how a child is responding to a teacher's efforts to build new skills and expand comprehension. Summative data, even when received in a timely manner, reveal little that directly affects the teaching/learning process.

Disaggregating data by gender and ethnicity, and by comparing the performance of children classified as special education or ELL against those who are not, helps to reveal generic performance patterns and disparities between groups. While well-intended, these data too are essentially useless to the practitioner who must expose the underlying root causes for a lack of learning within each student.

Even where states disaggregate student data based upon the percent passing or meeting a standard criterion for a certain skill or concept, the data do not reveal why the student struggled with the area reported. The best data reveal patterns and trends on a group level of analysis. Such data shed light on what is going on systemically but not why.

Multiple data sources would be required such as student and parent interviews to reveal the strengths and growth needs of individual students. Teachers have to discover what they can do to differentiate instruction for children. Teaching is the art of helping individual children to master a skill or knowledge base. Tests do not measure the quality of strategies for instruction, teacher dispositions, and the openness of interactions between a teacher, parent, and child.

Some schools hire consultants who take the school's state data and reorganize and disaggregate the data in multiple, highly customized ways. Ironically, this is most often the case in school systems with significant resources where meeting standards or AYP is rarely a problem. These consultants produce detailed data reports resplendent in lovely binders with glossy paper and colorful charts.

One wonders why even within these better districts with access to detailed data reports, teaching and learning rarely produce outstanding mastery performance for large percentages of the students.

The data generally reveal that even in school systems with adequate resources and supportive communities, the majority of their students are meeting proficiency. The vast majority of students are not achieving mastery levels of performance.

Systemic reliance on standardized test data by administrators and teachers does not improve schools. This is particularly true when the form of the data and the lag time between a test and the data report render the data virtually unusable for improving the teaching and learning process.

Add to the mix teachers and supervisors who have had little training in the use of data to inform instruction, and the preponderance of the evidence suggests that school systems, even those purported to be very good, tend to relax once all students meet proficiency.

We need a better system of collecting data from multiple sources that promotes mastery performance for all children in all curricula.

DESIGNING DATA SYSTEMS THAT HELP GROW STUDENT ACHIEVEMENT

School systems can improve the capacity of all children to learn if they acquire and analyze both summative and formative data from multiple sources. Teacher and school leaders need timely and useful data to regularly measure the instructional system's output. Such data analysis and processes continuously propel the system and its constituents toward achieving their goals.

When student data are empirical and anecdotal, quantitative and qualitative data are produced. By including multiple mixed methodologies to collect data, teachers have standardized test data, interview data, archival data, and portfolio data to inform them about student progress. The unifying factor is that the data reveal what teachers need to recognize to guide student growth.

School leaders know that children are successful when they are safe, nurtured, and held to high expectations by highly trained, dedicated educators who believe that failure is not an option. Such teachers use every resource at their disposal to insure that no child simply meets standards. They want all of their children to exceed state standards.

Successful school systems train faculty, staff, and leaders continuously. Training focuses directly on increasing teacher capacity to meet goals. Successful schools focus on teaching students well. Their data confirm this focus.

Leaders of successful schools align curriculum, supervision, and professional development with the district vision, mission, and goals. Leadership in effective schools is distributed among all stakeholders, particularly the teachers. In school settings that focus on every student's success, teachers collaborate regularly. They help each other to help every child succeed.

Using collaboratively designed, uniform assessments that align with both the standards and local goals, successful teachers use these assessments to guide instruction. These teachers and school leaders design programs that measure progress relentlessly. They know that a child who reads well, understands mathematics well, and who can think critically will not struggle with any standardized test.

W. Edwards Deming, widely considered the father of the continuous improvement movement, contended that systems that work use errors as opportunities to learn and avoid excuses that sustain an unacceptable failure rate (Walton, 1986). We can infer from his teachings that one should create data systems that measure student and faculty progress towards district goals. Data systems should guide teacher capacity to constantly improve the teaching and learning processes.

Systemic data collection and analysis should focus on processes that encourage teacher leadership. Professional development should align with the district mission and goals, promote ethical behavior, and influence the actions that teachers and school leaders take to grow student achievement.

ASSESSING YOUR CURRENT REALITY

Leaders, particularly in a high-stakes testing environment, are under tremendous pressure to raise test scores. The gap between current student achievement and the vision the system holds for future achievement is the fertile ground for creativity. Without a baseline of current achievement, one cannot measure growth. Without a vision, one cannot know what success looks like. Without both a baseline and a vision, a leader cannot establish expectations for growth and performance in the future.

TAKE OFF YOUR ROSE-COLORED GLASSES

Confronting your current reality honestly is critical to the change process. Any changes designed upon a faulty foundation are doomed to fail. Collins's plea that organizations confront the brutal, factual truth about what they believe and how they behave should echo throughout school systems (2001).

There are times when some system behaviors are less than flattering. It is best to start out expecting some embarrassing findings about the success of some students, and set ground rules that separate a quest for truth from a blame game.

School leaders, who blame others for unsatisfactory student performance, build their own barriers to success. The first stone cast toward the "responsible party(s)" creates an avalanche of fear and mistrust. Any inquiry the leader hoped to initiate has been doomed to failure by introducing fear into the dialogue.

Current reality, whether perceived as good, bad or somewhere in between, is a system issue. By that we mean it is an issue which reflects structural designs and culture—the way the system and its members organize attitudes, beliefs, and assumptions—as well as the delivery systems that reinforce beliefs that produce the outcomes.

If anything is to blame, it is most likely the system itself. One individual worker or teacher rarely causes the results of many individuals to reflect a pattern of continual errors. The point of confronting brutal truth is for everyone to look in the mirror and start a rich, professional dialogue that leads to an honest assessment of systems, culture, structures, and outputs.

Through this honest and deep introspection, one sees quite clearly what is working well and also if a system's espoused beliefs are barriers to change. Current policies and programs may be beneficial or may produce outcomes that are 180 degrees from the intended result. Sometimes school leaders carry the barriers in their heads with mental models that prevent them from seeing opportunities to change (Senge, 2000).

For instance, many educators state that they believe that "all children can learn." An exploration of system artifacts and beliefs may reveal a belief that "all children can learn, *but* . . ." At times, school leader commentaries reveal a long list following the "but" of excuses and explanations that justify current results and characterize them as the best possible outcomes. Such school leaders need to change or be changed.

Effective schools know what their purpose and values are. They are understood and embraced by all stakeholders. In effective schools, school leaders and teachers walk their talk. Ineffective schools have teachers and school leaders who talk and talk, their conversations peppered with "buts." In the case of the schools where the recurring commentary reflects: "We believe all children can learn, but . . ." one usually sees tracking structures are pervasive. Performance disparities between children in various disaggregated groups are dramatic and tolerated. It would not be shocking to find faculty chatter in ineffective schools reflect a statement such as: "Some of these kids just are not college material," or "Some of *them* will *never* get it!"

In school systems that work for *all* children, there is an unwavering belief that all children can learn at mastery levels. In these schools, the adults take responsibility for student success. Any perceived learning difficulty affects teaching strategies, not teacher expectations for success. All students are taught a rigorous curriculum and are held to high standards of achievement. Leaders and faculty must confront clearly who the students are with pre-ordained failure designations if they intend to improve achievement for all students.

YOU REAP WHAT YOU SOW

The real, brutal truth that schools must face is that a system can only produce the outputs and behaviors that it was designed to create. Whether intentional or not, one reaps the results that a system is designed to achieve. Leaders are responsible for the design of all systems, not the workers (Deming, 1994).

It is more difficult, yet not impossible, to see the brutal truth if you are engaging in self-reflection solely with people who live within your organization. Skilled and perceptive observers, particularly those who do not dwell within your system, may help to spot the dissonance between what is done and what is espoused.

Constant introspection, designed to gauge whether their efforts are producing the desired results, is a hallmark of effective schools. More importantly, when they find dissonance between the outputs they are seeking and what they efforts yield, they engage in deep inquiry before taking action.

School systems that work for *all* children do not overreact to events. Rather, they seek to identify patterns of behavior and engage in deep dialogue to identify the root causes that contribute to their disappointing results. Doctors and nurses are trained to identify underlying causes for symptoms. They apply effective healthcare strategies to diagnose disease and prescribe appropriate interventions. Effective health care providers recognize that a cure lies in isolating the actual disease and its source. They treat the disease and eradicate it so that the symptoms cannot reappear. In schools, effective educators identify the barriers to learning and find strategies to overcome those barriers with each child.

Without being open to objective feedback, all of us tend to lose perspective. We cannot see the forest for the trees. Organizationally, we replay the elements contained in the parable about a frog in boiling water. We decline so slowly, and comfortably, that we fail to recognize that our actual death is imminent.

If we wait too long to conduct an authentic assessment of current reality, we may be too weak and powerless to change the outcome.

School systems that work for all children continually evaluate their progress in real time. The data points that such schools use include external feedback that guide their improvement efforts. School systems that continuously improve seek feedback from colleges about their graduates, consult with employers about opportunities and preparation of high school graduates for the work force, and interview or survey students and parents about how well they were prepared for post-high school opportunities.

SEPARATING FACT FROM FICTION

Strong diagnostics must be designed into a school system. They should align with the mission and values of the school community. Assessment programs should identify emerging patterns of behavior that are discussed deeply by and with all relevant stakeholders. Without pertinent and timely data, teachers fall into the trap of reacting to every unusual event in school. Perhaps an example would prove helpful.

Five years earlier, prior to the arrival of Principal Jones at ABC Elementary School, the administration and faculty considered and adopted a new reading program. The prior leadership thought that the old reading program was not producing the outcomes they expected. Scores were flat. They began their search for newer and better materials. They learned of a new reading series that was considered the best available and very popular in their region. Teachers were excited about the change because the new series reflected the best practices, was research-based, and had supporting technology. It also came complete with promises of increased student achievement.

Teachers found the program and the materials easy to use. Feedback was all positive, and the series was adopted. Even better, it appeared that after the first year of implementing the program, scores were slowly creeping upward. The faculty saw progress but Principal Jones was concerned. Twenty percent of her students were still failing to meet standards, and the number of students at or above proficiency was extremely low.

Principal Jones felt that perhaps she should look at things differently. She read about Dr. Edwards Deming's use of Shewhardt's *Control Charts* (1994).

Using a control chart detailing ELA scores, she and her leadership team decided to look at how their students had improved over the course of the last ten years. They decided upon a ten-year look because it would reflect how students behaved in the old reading system and the new reading series.

Using archival data and the control charts, she noted that the mean number of students reaching proficiency or higher over the last ten years in her school was 80 percent. After discussing and analyzing the results, Principal Jones and her leadership team were satisfied, and particularly proud, given that their school was in a relatively "high-need" community. However, they also recognized that, on average, 20 percent of the student body was unable to reach proficiency, even within the last two years. This was truly upsetting to everyone.

Teachers thought the new reading series was quite good, though the data indicated that the standardized scores had not changed significantly. For teachers to see that, on average, 20 percent of their children were being left behind year after year was shocking. One of the team members asked, "Wait a minute, weren't the scores over the last five years showing a generally upward trend?"

Statistically, a control chart provides data about upper and lower control limits over time in addition to the mean. While the formula that mathematically computes control limits is somewhat complicated and unnecessary for our discussion, we want, for the purposes of our discussion, to think of upper and lower control limits as one standard deviation (+ or -) from the mean score reflecting the percent of students achieving proficiency. This is a workable assumption, not technically correct, yet it will serve as a means to explain our point.

Principal Jones's team saw that while the mean passing percentage was 80 percent, it was a function of the fact that in each of the last ten years scores sometimes went up, while in others, scores went down, but they never went above or below the statistically established upper or lower control limits. This would indicate that despite the new reading series and the perception of slightly improving scores, scores stayed within the range of the upper and lower control limits, and were essentially stagnant. This is the quintessential indicator of the status quo.

The variance of any data point within the upper and lower control limits is said to be a result of "common causes." In other words, this variance is to be expected and predicted. The fluctuations in scores each year were the result of common factors, like one grade level performed slightly better than the prior grade; or, the test was given in the middle of flu season; or, one year it was rainy and another, sunny.

These are things that are beyond the control of school personnel, and not extreme enough to cause a score to spike beyond the upper or lower control limits.

When a score pierces the upper or lower control limits, this is labeled a "special cause." As you would infer, special causes are uncommon and therefore require investigation and explanation. Much like statistical outliers, special causes skew data.

Assume the data point falls below the lower control limit. In a less skilled system, panic ensues and the blame game starts. We could even see a major shift in policy or program—perhaps still another new reading program. Leaders in effective systems resist immediate reaction and move faculty analysis to more profound inquiry.

Sometimes "special causes" are easy to spot. For instance, one year the vast majority of students in New York State, including honors and AP students, failed the Regents exam in Physics. Obviously, in this case the test was poorly constructed and scores had to be curved. An easy test might have the opposite effect. Scores are dramatically inflated and students look more proficient than they actually are.

In another instance, on the date of a test's administration, a popular faculty member suddenly died and his students were distraught. Scores might fall below the lower control limit because of student grief and lack of concentration. In these examples, we can pretty much pinpoint the special cause. Other times, we have to drill down much more deeply, and the reasons are more subtle.

Let's go back to our earlier example wherein Mrs. Jones revealed to the faculty that the mean passing rate for ten years was 80 percent. Almost all student scores were within the upper and lower control limits. Principal Jones observed that the system for teaching and learning, including the new reading series, produced this effect. The school is in "statistical control." Wheatley (2006) would state that this system has found "equilibrium."

A mean of 80 percent proficiency, over time, indicates that this is this system's comfort zone. It is producing the outcome it is designed to create with remarkable consistency. This is pretty powerful statistical evidence that a school system, its culture, as well as systemic structures, produce proficiency for only 80 percent of its students. Unfortunately, on the other hand, the learning system is designed so that year after year, 20 percent of the students fail. This is unacceptable under any circumstance.

Tinkering with issues, particularly in the absence of honest, reliable, and unfiltered data gained through collaborative dialogue and discovery, is a fix that fails. No amount of tinkering with program, curriculum, or schedules will change the systemic performance enough to raise the mean score over time. Everyone involved in this school system needs to rethink what they are doing and why they are doing it.

The problem does not lie within the reading series: it lies within the system itself. The design of the system and the beliefs about teaching, learning, reading instruction, and the capacities of the children drive a system.

Confronting current reality is the first step toward substantively changing a system culture and its output. This is not an easy process, and it can get out of control quickly if people within a school system do not have the capacity to adjust their mental models and be open to learning.

The greatest disability an organization can have is being unable to conduct deep, civil discourse around issues that matter. If this is the case in your system, some preparatory work may be in order before delving deeply into current reality. This is where a facilitator could be helpful.

DRILL DOWN AND GET BELOW THE SURFACE

Examine problems deeply, especially ones that have widespread implications for the system's long-term viability and success. Require honest, data-informed assessments from every possible angle and through the lens of every stakeholder.

As Collins (2000) stated, to truly transform a system, leaders must confront the brutal facts about current reality. This is the first step towards transforming an organization. Transformation takes time, patience, trust, perseverance, and a sustainable commitment to learn and grow.

The key to assessing your current reality is recognizing patterns of behavior, good or bad, and then delving deeply into inquiry to explain what is causing these behaviors to persist?

The control chart discussed previously helped Principal Jones to recognize a pattern of behavior that, upon reflection, was very troubling. To understand why a trend exists, one must delve more deeply into the system and the culture that enables the performance trend in the first place.

One of the best conceptual tools to understand an issue deeply is "The Iceberg" (Senge et al., 2000, p. 80). What is visible above the water's surface is important to see and recognize, yet what lies below the surface is critical and even essential to see.

Remember, the captain of the *Titanic* saw the iceberg. What he failed to realize and what was difficult to see were the parts of the iceberg that were below the surface. The ship's impact with the unseen, irregular structures of the iceberg concealed by the water, ultimately, sank the ship. The Titanic metaphor serves to remind us that what cannot readily be seen is exactly what needs to be seen in order to improve schools.

Senge (2000) and his colleagues see four questions as the starting point for systemic inquiry:

1. Event(s): What just happened?
2. Patterns/Trends: What has been happening?
3. Systemic Structures: What are the forces at play contributing to these patterns?
4. What about our thinking allows this situation to persist?

Using the *Iceberg* as a guide, when an event occurs, inquire as to what happened and address it rapidly and appropriately. As we like to say, if there is a fire, put it out. This is not the time to convene a committee.

However, if fire turns into a pattern of fires, there is something that we are not readily seeing that causes them. If a system or school has a disappointing pattern for student behavior, that is the time for a collaborative assessment.

Emergent patterns should be investigated using multiple lenses with diverse personnel. When an event turns into a pattern, leaders of effective school systems know that the underlying cause is systemic and that the cause lies within the structures and beliefs of the system.

Assume your school consistently made Adequate Yearly Progress (AYP) of 10 percent growth for all students in English Language Arts (ELA) for the first three of the last five years. This year, you have a bad result on a standardized ELA test used by your state to determine your schools NCLB status. Harking back to the control chart, you ask: "Is this event due to a common cause or a special cause?" Of course, we need to understand this event and, if it is a special cause within our control, fix it.

However, let's assume that this event represents the third year in a row that your scores declined, and the aggregate score fell below the mean for the past five years. This is a disturbing pattern, which, if not understood and addressed, could result in your school being labeled as "failing." The key here is to understand the pattern, and resist identifying "one" action as the solution.

Someone on your team points out that the data suggest that poor performance by Special Education students seems responsible for your scores falling. The observation may be true but it doesn't explain *why* this group's achievement is declining. What other patterns or trends exist that might clarify what is at play here?

Using multiple domains, we might look at the issue through the lens of teaching, learning, curriculum, culture, external forces, demographics, finance, beliefs, and policy. In essence, think of the event as a ball placed in a cube with multiple holes placed in all six sides. Each hole represents one of the domains described above. Peer through each hole to gain new insights into the patterns supporting this event.

At the systemic structural level, we ask, "What are the forces at play contributing to these patterns?" Here again, we seek to identify the structures that may have contributed to these patterns. Peering at the patterns through the same cube, what structures support or enable these patterns to arise? For instance, you might look through the lens of scheduling or staffing.

At the foundation of the *Iceberg* is Mental Models. An organization's attitudes, beliefs, assumptions, and rituals comprise its collective mental model or culture. In a root-cause analysis, we attempt to identify what about our thinking led us to create the systemic structures that produced the patterns and trends in performance/behavior that we identified as problematic?

Examining issues like this is potentially time-consuming but, as stated before, sometimes one must go slow to go fast. Seek a far deeper understanding of the multiple forces at play that cause systems to produce unwanted outcomes. Solutions that emanate from this deeper understanding begin to shift culture. School cultural solutions tend to be high-leverage and sustainable when they are generated by a team of committed educators.

Our purpose here is simply to help you see the deep issues that create the behaviors and outcomes schools produce. Again, if you cannot see the problem clearly, whatever solution you employ will have little effect on changing the system's ability to produce different results. We all need to be reminded that schools are living systems embodied by people.

If you take a school and remove all of the people, you simply have a building, usable for just about any purpose. It is the people, their purpose, and their interactions that cause the building to be defined as a school. All leaders should remember, particularly when assessing an issue or problem, that the people in the school and the parents possess the insights to guide sustainable change.

All issues and problems in schools are the result of the system's culture. Since everyone operates in a system, all must assume responsibility for its performance. Individual teachers are not to blame for the design of systems at a school. Leaders at the school have responsibility for the design of the system. The good news is that it is our mental models and assumptions that often cause the problems we face. By thinking differently, we can emerge better and stronger than ever before.

ARE YOU READY TO CHANGE?

As we move closer toward action, it pays to remind our readers that any actions taken to change a system without regard to culture—its beliefs, how it behaves, existing relationships, its awareness and sensitivity about issues at hand—are likely to fail. Any and all actions taken must explicitly consider the people, their culture and their preparedness to make the changes required.

Figure 3.1 describes what Peter Senge originally explained as "Domain of Enduring Change" (Senge, 1990). We like to think of this simply as representing a school's "Culture."

We could describe a culture as what members truly believe and how members behave. Senge (2004) offers a visual rendition of this definition. See Figure 3.1: Culture.

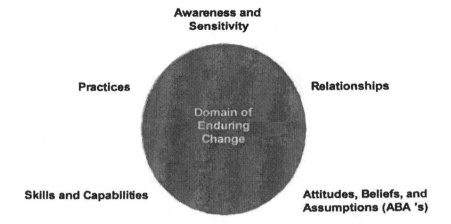

It's All About Culture

Figure 3.1.

By understanding the interrelationships of five factors deeply, we begin to understand exactly what the cultural beliefs are as well as how culture influences behavior. This analysis must consider both internal and external forces that affect the system's culture. These domains are not sequential and they frequently overlap.

The sum of the data collected allows school leaders to define culture clearly. To know culture deeply is essential for the introduction of change within an organization. By examining the elements of culture, a leader focuses on the strengths in the organization and how to capitalize on them.

1. Relationships: The sum and substance of an organization's culture is dependent on the quality of relationships and with whom they are established. Questions that come to mind include: Who are the formal and informal power brokers internally and externally? Who is "connected" to whom and how? What influence do community members have on Board of Education members? Do Board members have political aspirations and where do their loyalties lie? When someone does an "end-around" on the superintendent, who are typically the players and what are their relationships to each other? Relationships are to leadership as oxygen is to mammals.

2. Awareness and Sensitivity: This refers to an awareness of culture and the context within which personnel operate—sensitivity toward their own beliefs and practices and the effects they have upon the system.

What makes the organization tick? How in tune are people about the need to change? Is the internal culture attuned to the external culture? If not, where is the dissonance? Are we aware of "best practices" or are we comfortable with our current reality?

3. Attitudes, Beliefs, and Assumptions: This refers to what the culture holds as its "truth." Assume we wish to change from one reading series to another. What are the faculty attitudes towards the current reading system as well as the one under consideration? What are their beliefs about reading instruction? What assumptions does the culture inculcate in teachers about their students, parents, and reading instruction? Listen to the stories the teachers tell and the culture appears. Do you hear things like, "Here we go again. Another new administrator—another new reading program?" Pursue the cultural beliefs through inquiry. (Assess the gap between what teachers say they believe and what the artifacts, evidence, and data reveal.) Open a dialogue and keep the data transparent.

4. Practices: Investigate how the system actually works and how it aligns with what teachers say they believe. For instance, you may find they espouse a belief that all children have the capacity to learn at high levels yet their master schedules include tracking and many pull-outs for students from class to remediation centers.

5. Skills and Capabilities: If you are trying to implement change, this is where you assess the system's capacity to change and its preparedness for change.

BEWARE THE CULTURE OF EQUILIBRIUM

The concept behind the creation of charter schools is to cast aside that which does not work in our present schools and design schools that are better. In theory, we try to accomplish this by freeing charter schools from the shackles of certain mandates, rules, and regulations. Ironically, after years of experimentation, most charter schools look, feel, and perform today much like the public schools they compete against (Blake, 2008).

The data produced by these charter schools often reveal the same or worse results than public schools of similar size and grade configurations obtain. Constant results illustrate the power that our mental models and culture have over the design of schools, and the tendency to create anew what feels familiar.

If you had lived in a cave for the last twenty years and unknowingly toured a typical charter school, even though they often can cherry-pick their students, faculty, staff, and curriculum, you would generally walk out the door thinking that this school is pretty much like all of the others you remembered.

Not surprisingly, most charter school personnel hold the same attitudes, beliefs, and assumptions about children, teaching, and learning as their non-charter school brethren. This is equilibrium at play. Whenever we are exposed to something new or different or confronted with obstacles or roadblocks, we often end up recreating those environments that we once associated with success.

The societal mental model of what schools are and how they typically behave is so powerful that it forms a gravitational force field called school culture that even so-called innovators find difficult to alter (Wheatley, 2006).

As leaders, we need to deeply understand the culture of schools and schooling or we risk placing ourselves and our children perpetually stuck in the past. If systems were easy to change, we would not have the problems we face today. Failed governance and school systems, educational gaps, extreme dropout rates among our high school students in the 20 largest cities of the United States, and growing violent crime rates among students can be altered by creating new learning systems. Some schools have created effective learning communities. All schools must find ways to create learning communities that include all of their students.

We can safely say that any quick fix for a complicated problem is usually a bad fix. The band aid approach is rarely sustainable and often treats the symptom, not the root cause (Weeks, 1996). Worse, any fix implemented without deeply understanding the culture would be applied in ways that harmed the system and failed to create a new system.

FINAL THOUGHTS ON DIAGNOSIS

Change begins with reliable data about the system one wishes to alter. The attitudes, beliefs and assumptions of the organization undergoing a change effort must be profoundly understood before change is initiated. Inquiry and discovery are the first steps that a change agent must take. We suggest a few inquiry paths to follow:

- Do personnel have a vision of success?
- Can they identify their mission? Does the mission amplify and reflect the vision?
- Is there a set of guiding ideas or principles that enable the vision and mission to come to life in the daily functions of the organization?
- Is there any evidence that would clearly demonstrate progress toward the vision and mission?

- Are there metrics measuring progress toward the vision and mission? What are their underlying values? If not clearly known, why not? If yes, how much progress has been made?
- Is your performance aligned with stated achievement targets? If not, why not? If so, why? How?
- Is everyone in the organization aware of the vision and mission? Do they believe in it? Do they live and breathe it? How would you know?
- Do the people presently have the capacity to successfully carry out the vision and mission?
- Are staff development efforts empowering the organization to achieve the vision and mission? Or are they detractors?
- Does your culture embrace or welcome change? If not, under what conditions might they welcome change?

The list can go on and on. The goal is to create a question path that illuminates the mental models of your system. Your task is to reveal what personnel truly believe about the system to which they belong.

Do the data reveal that personnel "walk their talk" or do they simply talk a good game? In effect, inquiry raises awareness about the status of the organization by engaging stakeholders in a dialogue about current reality.

By asking questions, leaders cue personnel to reflect and to sense what is of concern. Effective change agents employ fewer advocacies and more inquiry, and suffer less push-back than most change agents. Be prepared for differing points of view. In fact, embrace them all.

The richness of data gained through inquiry depends on the diversity of views expressed and supporting data collected. Change is the primary responsibility of leaders.

Change requires dialogue, listening, and caring behaviors from leaders. Change emanates from a shared vision, mission, goals, and beliefs.

Chapter 4

Planning for Change
Vision and Core Beliefs

Leaders change a school system by developing a capacity to see and deeply understand the internal and external factors influencing the system. Margaret Wheatley describes these factors as force fields (Wheatley, 2006). Force fields simply exist and exert pressures.

Internally, force fields may emanate from parents, students, faculty and staff, administrators, teacher unions, informal leaders, or the Board of Education. Externally, force fields might include the commissioner of education, the Board of Regents, the federal government, unfunded mandates, fiscal issues, community issues, and other external pressures that influence events within schools.

Leading is complicated. Leaders who understand complexity, and who are aware of patterns of pressure surrounding them, are among the most successful. Warren Bennis (1999) described leadership as herding cats, and aptly noted how difficult it is to get a group of people to share a common vision, a mission and values.

An important step in leading change is to recognize that one must go slowly to go fast. This sounds like heresy in the "hurry up and improve" environment that educators now seem to work within. However, an effective leader prepares an organization for sustainable success. Success is imbedded within a well-designed vision, taught to the organization, and supervised with a laser-like focus (Senge, 1999).

Michael Fullan observed that change initiatives become stymied by an implementation dip where phenomena exhibit a rise in short-term target results, followed by a dip in those same results as staff recognizes the extra effort that new work requires. The implementation dips in the results scare inexperienced leaders. Often, they are the first to abandon the change effort prematurely.

Inexperienced leaders fail to understand that change comes with organizational chaos, confusion, and cynicism within the ranks of employees. There is always a short rise and a dip in results as enthusiasm for the new work wanes. As change initiatives stall, effective leaders engage in deep inquiry and learn what needs to be adjusted to achieve the goals. They become more reflective. They are more determined to find effective solutions. They execute plans, and do so in ways that are more flexible than rigid.

Flexibility requires courage. Courage is a balance between bravery and foolhardiness (Aristotle) that requires prudent use of data and collaborative inquiry. The chance of success one has with current efforts is under constant scrutiny. Success is never guaranteed. Successful endeavors grow exponentially when decisions are informed by data and reflect a deep sensitivity to culture. Discussions must be thoughtful, safe, truthful, collaborative, and collegial if the process is to change the culture.

LEADERSHIP BELIEFS

The school leader's clear understanding about the purpose of education, how children learn, and a vivid and detailed vision of the desired school guide transformation of the organization. School leaders should understand their own motives and values. They must be comfortable expressing core beliefs and non-negotiable values.

Core beliefs and non-negotiable values are those that one holds so dear that they cannot be abandoned. If a leader states that a non-negotiable value is "Always place children first," then each decision, policy, and directive should be considered in terms of the best interests of children.

If a leader states a core belief that everyone in the organization should be treated with dignity and respect, then every action a leader takes or conversation a leader has should convey this belief. Such leaders oppose treating someone else, whether a child or an adult, with anything less than dignity and respect. Even the most disagreeable employee or constituent must be treated with dignity and respect.

As a leader, the way one behaves says more about leader expectations for others and the type of school one leads than any words a leader may speak.

The second step in a change initiative that a leader should take is to compare what the leader believes and what the organization's personnel believe. Where is there alignment or misalignment? Where might there be agreement or disagreement? Where is the leader willing to be flexible and open to influence? How should a collaborative vision of the new school be developed?

How shall the leader bring diverse groups, internally and externally connected to the school, together to forge a new vision?

Effective leaders might ask themselves: Do I have the capacity to lead the desired change? If not, who does, and can I count on them? Does the organization have the capacity to successfully achieve the desired change? If not, what preparatory steps need to be taken to make the organization embrace a need for change? The questions should be customized to one's individual culture and organizational needs.

We can tell you this with certainty. The best place to start your assessment is usually by looking in the mirror. The next place is the organizational mirror. By comparing the two side by side, a leader can gain a good sense about where and with whom to begin change efforts. At the outset, leaders have to decide what to emphasize, and with which groups to work.

CREATING A NEW VISION

In these times of fiscal uncertainty, it is critical that schools have a long-term vision. School systems that work for all children bring together all stakeholders associated with the school community and, together, build a clear vision for student success. Their vision is the guidepost that influences their school's mission, guiding ideas and goals. All of their innovative structures are designed around their vision which influences every aspect of their culture—what they believe and how they behave.

In effective school systems, everyone works hard to develop individual and collective capacity to enable the vision and mission to come to life. Effective school systems explicitly align their governance systems, policies, hiring and supervision practices, budget, curriculum, pedagogy, staff development, and decision-making with their vision and mission.

Leaders of school systems that work for all children use vision and mission as a compass for every component of the system's actions and design. They use data to establish baselines and benchmarks that indicate progress towards goals. They organize data into information that informs decisions for continuous short- and long-term academic growth.

In school systems that work for all children, data collection methods are designed to illuminate how well the system is moving toward achieving its stated vision, mission, and goals. Data are both formative and summative. Data informs all decisions in the central office, the principal's office, every classroom, and even the custodian's office.

If decisions are inconsistent and do not align with the system's stated purpose, the organization quickly recognizes the dissonance. Stakeholder reaction is quick and widespread because the decision conflicts with the attitudes, beliefs, and assumptions that the system and its people collectively hold for themselves.

Data-driven systems adjust quickly. Thus, nothing gets too far out of alignment. The system stays on course to meet its vision, mission, and goals. Leaders in school systems that work realize that data are not owned and understood only by those at the top of the organizational chart. In a school system where leaders are serious about leading with vision, their inquiry and dialogue center on open access to the data that reveal how well the schools are doing.

Everyone needs to have a sense of whether the mission is being accomplished or not. Data inform all decisions, and every decision propels the system another step closer to realizing the collective vision and mission.

Proper data analysis requires student, program, curricula, personnel and facility data that reveal trends in at least three year cycles. Data should identify strengths and weaknesses. Opportunities lie among weaknesses. They lead to informed options and the selection of valued alternatives.

VISION AND MISSION—DO YOU SEE WHAT I SEE?

Before discussing prescriptions for success, we need to say a few words about vision and mission. Effective schools construct their practice upon a strong vision and a clear mission. There are few school systems in our country that have not created a vision or mission statement proclaiming their values about educating their children.

In some states, having a mission statement is even a requirement. Of course, whether required or not, there is no guarantee that employees will adopt the vision and mission. Few employees can recite, and fewer can explain, the vision or mission. We do not see vision and mission as synonymous. One is necessary for the other to be operable. Both statements must be clear and deeply understood by employees or the system will not be successful.

Visioning is a concept long used by the greatest athletes and artists of our time. Tiger Woods, arguably the greatest golfer of our time, uses visioning extensively. He takes the time to create a mental picture of success on multiple levels. He pictures his success on all 18 holes before beginning a round. He envisions the optimal means of playing each hole. Before taking any shot, he analyzes his lie and the distance to the green, observes potential hazards, and evaluates his options. Tiger then confers with his caddie and ascertains his view of the shot. Once settling on his best option, he engages in a series of practice swings, all the time envisioning the perfect swing necessary to place the ball exactly where he wants it to land and where it will roll to a stop. His mission is clear: win every tournament. Yet, to win every tournament he must see success in every hole, swing, or putt he takes. We could say that his vision is his picture of success or the mental blueprint that guides him toward the fulfillment of his mission.

In schools, we rarely take the time to dream about what our success would look like. We need to create a vision of success in 3-D, one that all stakeholders can see. We get so caught up in the barriers to our success that we lose sight of our core purpose: To educate all children to the highest levels of learning necessary for productive citizenship in our twenty-first century democracy.

Assume for the moment, that you accept as one of your core beliefs that your purpose as an educator is "to educate all children to the highest levels of learning necessary to thrive in our twenty-first century democracy." Several questions should arise. First, what exactly does this mean? Second, what will this "look" like when we have such a school? Without vision, there is no context for the mission. Without a vision, we have no means to see the world we aspire to create for our children, faculty, staff, leaders, and the communities we serve.

Mission statements should align to our vision. They serve the purpose of taking our picture of success and setting it into words that describe what we value. A mission reflects content, purpose, and criteria for success. The mission statement forms the foundation for systemic design. The mission statement is what we assess.

Mission statements vary in size and scope. Some speak to what the parents and students are responsible for. Some speak to how the school and the children will be successful. Other mission statements speak to how the school takes responsibility and ownership for the education of its children. Almost all have some phrase proclaiming to help all students "achieve success in the twenty-first century."

Most schools post their mission statements in public areas, like the main lobby, the Principal's office, and the district Web site. Without debating the merits of any particular mission statement, one thing is usually true: few employees have any idea about what their mission statement proclaims, its intended meaning, or even where it is located. Do not hold your breath trying to find anyone who can recite it.

When you do find the rare birds that can recite the school's mission statement, have some fun asking them what it actually means and what steps the school or system has taken to enable their stated mission to come to fruition.

Having a mission statement is often perceived as unavoidable. For many educators, the mission statement represents an obligatory compliance issue rather than an important act that has practical and tangible purpose. Researchers and scholars rarely find a connection between a school's stated mission (espoused theory) and what they actually do (theory-in-use) (Argyris and Schön, 1978). Universally, schools rarely measure what the mission statement indicates they value for themselves, their students and community (Wiggins and McTighe, 2007).

Effective schools have a collaborative, inclusive process designed to create a clear, detailed picture of the school system's vision of success. They have a well-articulated mission statement. They represent the first building blocks of systemic change within a school.

The mission should be based upon a clear and compelling vision. The mission serves as the rudder that allows a school system to stay on course and navigate through both calm and rough seas. Data-informed decision-making is the propeller driving a school ever closer to fulfilling its vision and mission. Effective schools have a clear and well-known vision and mission.

VISION AND MISSION ARE NOT SYNONYMOUS

As Rich began to serve as superintendent of a large, suburban school district that New York State Education Department classified as "low wealth/high need," a new commissioner of education was appointed. The standards movement in New York State changed from a Compact for Learning to a Contract for High-Stakes Tests.

Rich felt that students in his system were capable of higher achievement. He agreed wholeheartedly with the need to raise the bar for all students. He saw this statewide shift in governance as an opportunity to begin a discussion with his leadership team about his school district's culture. He asked questions about system structures and how well they aligned with the new standards.

After conducting a team effort to study the new standards, it quickly became apparent to his leadership team that the picture of student success that they held for themselves was simply incompatible with the new standards. The school system celebrated unique successes and allowed too many minimum-performance results.

In the low-stakes, minimum-competency environment his school personnel had been trained to accept, many believed that they were highly successful. However, in the new, more rigorous high-stakes testing environment they were entering, problems emerged.

The biggest problem of all was that the staff held a vision of the school system as one that performed beautifully as it was. In fact, in their minds, they were doing well and had the data to prove it. Recently, their schools had been honored and received the U.S. Department of Education Blue Ribbon Award three times, three New York State Schools of Excellence awards, the most outstanding music program in the nation by the Music Educators National Conference, and many other local, state, and national accolades and awards.

In fact, his school community, like most others, met the standards movement with the usual cynicism and contempt reserved for most change initiatives that required forced compliance with little or no input from the practitioners or support from the teachers who had to do the new work.

Some of his district leaders realized that the standards movement had tangible benefits for the children and the system. The implementation and accountability imposed by NCLB challenged old assumptions about students whose academic performance fell in the lower half of the bell-shaped academic curve.

In some districts, teachers compared raising standards to raising high-jump bars to levels "short people could not clear." The "bell curve" which was intended to describe a normal distribution of behavior, attitude, or knowledge for a large group had become for them fixed quartiles into which all people should be slotted.

Once a student had been slotted inside a quartile, his or her achievement on academic standard exams was expected to remain in that quartile. School tracks were designed to keep children in their quartiles under the guise of "meeting their needs." Teachers referred to themselves by the student tracks in which they taught using phrases such as: I'm an Advanced Placement teacher, or I'm an Adjusted Track teacher.

When Rich raised questions about teacher assumptions regarding student performance, discontent and anger among faculty and staff appeared. Negative stereotypes began to surface about what their students were actually capable of producing, particularly academically. The need to change and faculty resistance to change were on a collision course with the new standards.

Aside from the usual fear associated with any change, no one could see student success as meaning that poor and migrant children should do as well as middle-class students in this school district. The roadblocks to change were social, emotional, and fiscal.

It became apparent that fighting the forces and holding onto the past was futile. Until the faculty and community could envision a new school system, changing the current reality would tear apart the system. Rich wondered what success would look like for a child graduating from his school system in the domains of academics, social and emotional literacy, the arts, and physical education.

This was not a job for one person, let alone someone who was a novice superintendent of schools.

Fortunately, Rich knew from experience that the further one climbs in a district's hierarchy, the more dependent one is upon others to do the actual work of implementing plans. This is particularly true when one hopes to implement change.

Always a believer in the power of collaborative processes, Rich knew that the task before him required even more communication, supervision, and clarity of purpose than ever before. If he and the district were to be successful, he had to engage in more dialogue than ever before.

Dialogue had to be focused on creating awareness about the paradigm shift that the schools faced. A new picture of success that everyone understood and supported had to be created. The new vision of student success needed to include a deep belief in student mastery of cognitive, social, and emotional states.

In 1996, Rich began by asking the school board what he thought was a simple question. "If we had no barriers to our success, what would a successful graduate of our school system know and be able to do upon graduation?" As was typical of his School Board, there was a professional and civil discourse. Board members had developed good listening skills, and a sincere desire to understand one another. There was little disagreement in general about the core purpose of educating children and improving the community. On a specific vision for all students, no distinct patterns of agreement or disagreement emerged.

Rich began to wonder what others thought and felt. He set about asking the same questions to administrators, teachers, parents, students, citizens without children in the schools, business people, and just about anyone else with whom he interacted.

Rich was often surprised that many individuals could not articulate precisely what they thought a graduate should know and be able to do academically, socially, emotionally, artistically, and physically. He was further amazed that the more discussions he had and the more feedback he received, the more refined, focused, and articulated his personal vision became.

He was learning that he needed to hold a community summit. He had to engage the community in articulating a new vision for their school district. As the community summit meetings progressed, people started to believe that they could control their own destiny, create their own vision of the future, and initiate change.

His constituents began to see him as a different kind of leader—one who cared deeply about the children, everyone's success, and someone who asked many questions, listened, processed, and responded to their answers.

The initial inquiry ultimately became a formal process of creating a collective vision—a widely-held mental picture of the success that the stakeholders wished to create for the system and the students it served. Because he and the Board wanted to participate in the process more deeply and engage the entire community more formally, the district hired a facilitator to host an event attended by over 400 people.

At the community summit, residents and employees were invited to express their "Wishes, Hopes, and Dreams" for their children and community. Only after they created the "picture" of success did they embark on the process of creating a Mission statement.

THE POWER OF THE MISSION STATEMENT

The stakeholders in Rich's district strongly believed that the vision and mission statement were the foundation on which schools had to be designed. They wanted every structure, program, decision, and data point referenced to, and aligned with, the stated mission of the school system.

Ideally, mission statements are living documents that reflect the best thinking of a collaborative group. They are referred to for guidance regularly and periodically reevaluated. They should not be empty, obligatory statements, compliantly written or devoid of context. They should not be hung on a wall or placed on a Web site and forgotten.

If well-written, mission statements can withstand the passage of time, and rarely require tweaking. They should not reflect the buzzwords or educational fads of the moment. They should be clear statements of the community's values and hopes for the children.

There is no right way to design and develop a viable mission statement. What is valued may, and probably will, differ somewhat from community to community. Many books contain wonderful advice about writing effective mission statements. Our best advice is to gather as much information as possible from as many sources as possible. Customize the process to your school system's culture and needs. Develop the mission statement in public.

In one school district, we observed school leaders use a community "blog" to construct a vision and mission statement in public forum. They shared Board of Education considerations, recommendations from the district committee for a new vision and collected feedback from community members who could not attend physical meetings. They orchestrated virtual and physical meetings to achieve a new vision and mission for their school system.

We advocate that the vision express a mental picture of what students will be able to do upon graduation. For instance, answer a question: how well-prepared will they be for a rapidly changing technological world? A mission statement developed in isolation and without a post-graduation context, however well-intentioned, is useless. In fact, it could be downright dangerous. A poorly-designed mission could sub-optimize your school system, and negatively affect those whom you graduate.

Your local vision and subsequent mission must reflect what your school system values on its journey towards preparing your students for post-graduate life. In other words, as Wiggins and McTighe (2007) recall, a mission statement must be created within a context and with a destination in mind.

Mission statements reflect the internal and external communities' wishes, hopes, and dreams for their children. The stated mission should influence curricula, program design, budget, supervision, and data collection. Mission statements influence virtually everything that makes up the intricacies of the place we call school.

A collaboratively-designed, thoughtful vision and the subsequent mission statement provide school systems with the leverage to change. All structural designs, teaching and learning events, and supervision promote systemic changes required for continuous learning.

A clearly articulated mission states what one values and seeks to achieve. District personnel design and implement systems that hold stakeholders accountable for what the system produces and the processes it uses to achieve the mission.

BRINGING YOUR MISSION TO LIFE

Many districts around the country have well-stated and carefully crafted mission statements; yet, there is little evidence that they have fulfilled them. This is often because they fail to take their mission statements to the next step: actualization. Mission statements, even good ones, often contain general statements of what a district values. Take this slice from the William Floyd School District's Mission Statement (1997) for example:

> We are committed to teach, encourage, and challenge all students to fulfill their intellectual, emotional, aesthetic, and physical potential, and to apply their knowledge and skills to become contributing, responsible citizens of a rapidly changing, diverse global society.

It sure sounds good. Who would not want to send their children to this school? The mission is not worth the paper it is written on unless steps are taken to actualize it—to bring it to life. So, the first typical question is, "How do we do it?"

First, start with revisiting the vision. Remember, this picture was or should have been the inspiration for the mission statement. Then, through inquiry and dialogue, stakeholders must define and teach the concepts embodied in the mission. We might ask several questions to start.

1. How are we defining "teach?" "Encourage?" "Challenge?"
2. How do we ascertain and define student potential?
3. What do we presently use to determine potential? Why is it valid and reliable? How do we know? What else should we use?
4. Is our current system focused on education as seen through a "world view" or a "local view?"
5. What knowledge and skills are required to be a good citizen of a rapidly changing, diverse global society? Where would we even begin to find this information?
6. How does our present culture model the ability to react to rapid changes in knowledge and skill?
7. How well does our present culture promote diversity?

These are simple questions with potentially very complicated answers. We are not taking the position that these are the "right" questions, although they very well may be. The point is to start with creating a common understanding of what the mission statement actually means for your culture. These are not the kind of questions one seeks answers to in a monthly 40-minute faculty meeting. Leaders must make time available for this discussion. Everyone must be willing to go slow in order to go fast.

Unfortunately, it seems that too few are willing, especially in this high-stakes testing environment, to deeply engage in these discussions. School leaders succumb to the pressures of the "quick fix." Obviously, you cannot let a school system crash and burn while you and your colleagues create a committee and ponder the universe. It is not a question of "either/or." Leaders have to conduct simultaneous and continuous efforts to maintain a functional system while planning and implementing its redesign and replacement.

DEFINE, THEN ALIGN

Even the simplest terms and concepts must be discussed and refined to build a new culture. The following statement, extracted from the same mission statement, required quite a bit of discussion in Rich's district. The stakeholders did not have a common definition or "picture" of what "nurturing" meant. The mission statement called for nurturing. It stated:

> Our mission will be achieved in a learner-centered, nurturing and safe environment, designed to empower students with the ability and desire to thrive as life-long learners.

This statement has an admirable goal. In the course of discussing the statement, a question was raised about what the word "nurturing" actually meant. Webster's New World Dictionary provides the following definitions: "1) to feed or nourish; and 2) to train, educate, rear." That definition seems pretty clear yet, through continued dialogue and discussion with staff, a different "working definition" emerged.

Given the difficult circumstances that many students faced socially and economically in the school district, the general interpretation held by many of the staff was that "nurturing" was synonymous with "empathizing." Teachers and other instructional support staff valued and encouraged empathy as virtuous behavior.

Since many children lived in very difficult circumstances, empathy was certainly a welcome, warranted, and very human first response. Yet, empathy alone would not be enough to help a child cope with life's circumstances. Certainly, empathy should not replace high expectations for academic and civic success.

Helping a child acquire the skills necessary to cope with or change one's environment required teachers who understood their role more deeply than being sensitive to student circumstances at home.

Teachers had to examine best practices available, and find ways to assist a child improve as a learner and cope with personal circumstances that hindered learning. In many cases, teachers had to discover new resources, new methods and new strategies to help their students. They had to deal with their students' family members. They had to raise their own, their students', and student family member expectations for academic success and school participation.

Finding the right metaphor to motivate almost all stakeholders to create the common understanding necessary to allow one word such as "nurturing" to guide all acts in a common and desired purpose seemed almost impossible.

Rich tried to apply basic learning theory to his school system. Using a concept espoused by Richard Strong (Strong, Silver and Perrini, 2001), the word "nurturing" was carefully examined in order to know and understand it deeply. Rich asked his staff to follow four steps in order to "own" the knowledge of "nurturing" that they sought.

1. Be able to define it (To feed; to teach or educate)
2. Be able to draw a picture (physically or mentally) of what a concept means (Picture how one nurtures a plant or garden)
3. Be able to draw a picture (physically or mentally) of what a concept *does not* mean (Picture a teacher empathizing with a sad child)
4. Define its attributes (teaching, learning, empowering)

This may seem like a very painstaking process. The results are worth the effort. Thriving organizations, in the private or public sector, work diligently and continuously to get everyone on the same page. If everyone has the same understanding of the organizational mission, the majority of the constituents will embrace it.

GUIDING IDEAS

Peter Senge defined guiding ideas as "the governing concepts and principles that define the way the organization exists, what we seek to accomplish, and how we intend to operate. It is the domain of purpose, vision, and values" (2006, p. 285).

If we deconstruct an existing mission statement, concept by concept, we have a good start at identifying its guiding ideas. Once guiding ideas are well-defined, we can begin developing, teaching, implementing, coaching, and monitoring for results.

Let us take the first part of the mission statement and place it in the form of several unique guiding ideas.

1. "We are committed to teach, encourage, and challenge all students to fulfill their intellectual potential"
2. "We are committed to teach, encourage, and challenge all students to fulfill their emotional potential"
3. "We are committed to teach, encourage, and challenge all students to fulfill their aesthetic potential"
4. "We are committed to teach, encourage, and challenge all students to fulfill their physical potential"

Each new guiding idea should reflect the desired future. The Mission Statement is reflective of the 360-degree view from 30,000 feet. It is the big picture.

The processes we describe may appear to be linear and somewhat formulaic. This is not our intention. In reality, this process is far more organic. If we were creating a new school, district, or initiative, we might begin with a vision and mission and then begin to identify guiding ideas. If we already have a defined mission, we might deconstruct it as outlined above to identify the guiding ideas.

Leaders must work through each step to create common understanding and buy-in. Guiding ideas can and should help transition a district's vision and mission from reflection to action.

FROM GUIDING IDEAS TO OPERATING PRINCIPLES

If we take our guiding ideas and place them into an "if-then" format, this will help to start the design process for our vision to come alive. Guiding ideas are the building blocks for behaviors, habits of mind, and programs that align with our stated mission and values. By placing guiding ideas into an "if-then" format, they become our "guiding principles" or "operating principles."

To make our Guiding Ideas operational we create "answers" to the "then" side of the equation within every applicable educational domain. Taking the first guiding idea as an example, the following represents one viable progression. The goal is to create the "then" part of the statement which addresses your new vision.

For this example:

If we are committed to teach, encourage, and challenge all students to fulfill their intellectual potential, then . . .

A. List implications for Learning
   a. We must teach so that all children acquire mastery in literacy by the end of third grade and maintain their mastery throughout high school
   b. We must teach so that all children acquire mastery in mathematics by the end of third grade and maintain their mastery throughout high school
B. List implications for Program Access and Opportunity
   a. We must develop programs and interventions that support and enhance efforts for all children to acquire mastery in literacy and mathematics by the end of third grade
   b. We must teach and tutor for mastery-level performance K–12
C. List implications for Support Services
   a. We must create support services that are child-centered, flexible, accessible, research-driven, and goal-focused
D. List implications for Curriculum

   a. We must design curriculum so that it emphasizes interdisciplinary outcomes, mastery in literacy and mathematics, creative and higher-order thinking skills

E. List implications for Teaching
   a. All instruction must be differentiated based upon individual student needs and learning styles
   b. All instructors must teach and develop higher-order thinking skills and creative endeavors
   c. All teachers must have the capacity to teach subject-specific reading and mathematics at mastery levels required for each subject

F. List implications for Supervision
   a. All administrators must have deep knowledge of curriculum, and the teaching and learning process
   b. All administrators must be collaborative leaders who value and demonstrate the tenets of servant leadership
   c. All administrators must evaluate school outcomes

G. List implications for Assessment
   a. We must collaboratively develop formal and informal assessments that align with our guiding ideas
   b. Assessments must be both formative and summative and designed to give the instructional faculty the information they need to improve each student's performance
   c. Assessments will establish individual student baselines, benchmarks and exit criteria

H. List implications for Professional Growth
   a. Teachers must be supported and coached, not judged and left to their own devices
   b. Professional Development must align directly with our goals and aspirations

I. List implications for Staffing
   a. We must hire leaders, faculty and staff who love children and value education
   b. We must hire leaders, faculty and staff who have the capacity to teach to our guiding ideas and achieve our goals
   c. We must hire leaders, faculty and staff who see our guiding ideas as minimal standards

J. List implications for Culture/Social/Emotional Literacy
   a. Every child and adult will be seen for their strengths and be treated with dignity and respect
   b. Social and emotional literacy will be a core component and integrated into every curriculum

K. Finance, physical space, scheduling, guidance services, and other domains need to explicitly define their role in insuring that the guiding ideas come to life

When everyone engages in building the "new story" of success, the process itself promotes collaboration and common understanding. This is not to suggest it is easy. We know that whatever decisions come from this process, they will be understood, and they will receive far greater support than they would were one to use the "see a problem-fix a problem" method.

INNOVATIVE INFRASTRUCTURES: GETTING TO "HOW"

If we accept Deming's notion that our school systems are producing the outputs they are designed to produce, then it makes sense that any change designed to elevate student achievement must create a different school system. In other words, leaders must not only innovate, they must enable new relationships and creative thinking of the faculty and staff to emerge.

Innovation requires a leader and a team to realize that structures presently in place are inadequate for the new mission. Educators might ask: "Does replacing one reading series with another count as innovation?" The short answer is probably not. A reading program in itself is rarely the problem. Moreover, if you roll out the new reading series in the same way you rolled out the last reading series, the likelihood of a failed change increases.

Taking a new packaged program or curriculum from any vendor could produce small changes in the performance of a school system. However, we know that adopting a new text rarely creates major improvements in student learning. New learning requires a deep examination of the issue related to student literacy. If a school recently purchased a new curriculum package, several questions should be asked to guide the implementation:

1. How much data have been gathered about the existing program?
2. Do we have data that inform us about the prior program's strengths and weaknesses?
3. Did we consider the users' beliefs about the prior series and the expectations for student performance?
4. Did we examine teachers' perceptions about reading and the capacity of the children they teach?
5. Did we create guiding ideas that informed the selection process? Are they aligned with our vision and mission?

6. Have we considered guiding ideas for ongoing professional development and coaching?
7. What new skills, knowledge, and tools must our teachers possess to have every child master independent literacy skills by grade three?

Absent substantive evidence that data were gathered about literacy efforts in the school and teacher beliefs about literacy, the textbook series will not make much of a difference. In many cases, time and money might be better spent teaching the faculty how to implement the existing program.

OPERATING PRINCIPLES LEAD TO INNOVATIVE INFRASTRUCTURES

Operating principles are essentially the blueprint that we use to design innovations and to assess their alignment with our goal. They reflect the *"then"* part of our statement. Let us step back to one of the Operating Principles we stated earlier:

> If we are committed to teach, encourage, and challenge all students to fulfill their intellectual potential, then we must teach and support all children to acquire mastery in literacy by the end of third grade.

School leaders start with inquiry and ask teachers how we can make this goal a reality. Teachers respond to questions about how all students can meet the goal of mastery in literacy in grade three. What would it take? What would instruction look like? How would our teaching change? How would our assessments change? How would instructional time shift?

The process of collaborative inquiry helps innovative infrastructures begin to emerge. A parallel inquiry should examine research and best practices for programs, curriculum, and teaching strategies that might help produce mastery in all students by the end of grade three.

This entire process, especially when collaborative, pays huge dividends because it represents the start of professional development.

We recommend repeating the same process with each operating principle. In essence, bring the "force" of the entire system to bear on innovative practices.

Let's look at another example which aligns with the aforementioned operating principle that all students achieve mastery in literacy by grade three.

Assume that your school system is consistently reporting that 75 percent of the students are scoring at or above proficiency on a standardized Grade 3 ELA assessment. Of the 75 percent at or above proficiency, only 25 percent are scoring at mastery levels. This means that only 25 percent of your students currently meet your operating principle. 75 percent of the students do not meet the school district standard for literacy at third grade. 50 percent perform at the proficiency or minimum standard and another 25 percent are below minimum standards.

Clearly, this mastery goal will not be met in one year, or even two. Based upon the readiness of the school culture, a gradual increase of the systemic tension over a period of time should occur, and all stakeholders should realize the gap between current reality and the mission of the school.

If you were to take six months to a year researching best practices and planning this initiative carefully, how much time would it take to show authentic growth in student mastery? If teaching and training of faculty and staff began in years two and three, and the new program opens with Kindergarteners, when would results be evident? Three years later? If one adds subsequent grade levels yearly, by the end of six years would almost all children achieve mastery in literacy by the end of third grade? Even if your results were somewhat short of this goal, think of the positive impact on students if mastery increased for more than half of the children. Recognize that it takes a long time for any culture to change substantively.

This is why school leaders must continuously educate the public and the board of education about the time required for substantive, sustainable change.

What is important to remember is not to allow any setbacks to deter you from your vision. Your vision and goals should be lofty. Collins (2001, p. 215) noted that all successful organizations create "Big Hairy Audacious Goals (BHAG's)." They serve to propel your system from equilibrium toward your vision of success.

If you get stuck along the way, for any reason, instead of modifying your aspirations, modify the timeline and consider how you will roll out improvements in this initiative. Learn from mistakes and challenges. Alter strategies; not vision. Provide clear evidence of substantive progress as soon as you can.

The key to success is to let your vision drive your mission and your mission drive your guiding ideas. Your guiding ideas should evolve into operating principles. Operating principles guide the innovations that are unique to your culture. In short, your vision must drive your design.

BE BRAVE AND PERSISTENT

Remember, the essential task in the entire change process is to re-imagine and transform your school system so that it produces the results you truly desire. When you get to the stage of transforming your guiding ideas into operating principles, the critics may come out in force. Be brave. Be patient, persistent, and personable. Continue to engage in inquiry, and stay true to your aspirations.

Follow a simple and clear pathway to success:

Teach for Success
Supervise for Success
Seek Evidence of Success
Set Appropriate Timelines
Work With People
Avoid the Quick Fix

Leaders are often challenged with solving complex problems immediately if not sooner. The pressure placed on leaders for answers and quick solutions, especially by the media and parents, is intense. No one wants to hear that you will look into a complex issue and get back to them. "Now" is the world in which we live and the timeline most constituents want for answers. Leaders guide them to higher levels of moral judgment by being patient, persistent, and personable.

Strong leadership is not about fighting fires. Heroic firefighters rush into burning buildings, save the victims, and extinguish the flames. Problem solved. Accolades are properly bestowed. Then, they go to the next fire. In contrast, the role of leadership is to find ways to prevent fires.

The reality is that leaders must put out fires when they have to, but their larger, more important role is to prevent fires from happening in the first place. This is clearly not as heroic or dramatic as running into a burning building. Leaders of schools that work for all children serve as the guardians of our children's future and of our democracy.

Many leaders have observed: "The pace of the decisions I need to make come at me like the speed of light." We have all felt: "I wish I had the luxury to reflect when everything seems to require my urgent attention." If this is the pattern of behavior in your school system as opposed to an occasional event, we submit that this may be a symptom of a systemic design flaw and a failure of leadership in your school.

As W. Edwards Deming proved time and time again, our systems produce the results and behaviors we design them to produce. "Ok," you say, "but the fire is still burning!"

When a critical situation arises, the internal and external constituents of the system demand immediate attention. They want action—now! In this case, effective leaders prescribe the leadership equivalent of an aspirin to treat the emergent symptom. They respond as expected. They know that deeper inquiry may be required to get at the core or root cause of the issue. A "root-cause" fix is where behavior shifts throughout the system.

The paradox that all leaders face is that they need to put out fires quickly, keep us safe, and simultaneously find ways to transform an old antiquated system into a new system. Effective leaders quickly understand that putting out the fire simply buys time—time to examine the "fire" and the issues around it more deeply.

Effective leaders know that by putting out the fire, they addressed a symptom and not the cause. The fire may reoccur and the root cause has not been addressed. If "everything is an emergency" in your school system, this is a strong indicator that the leadership team must engage in deep and thoughtful inquiry into how the system produces this constant sense of urgency. You need to resolve systemically why everything in your system feels like an emergency.

Leaders who mistake a quick fix for a permanent fix virtually assure that their system will fail to prosper, or worse, survive. School leaders who seek a quick fix and raise test scores for children by increasing test preparatory time train students to think they are not able to transfer knowledge to new situations. In fact, critical thinking and the capacity to learn in new situations may actually be stunted by test-prep activities.

What good are improved test scores if dropout rates continue at 25 percent of the nation's youth, and in some regions, significantly exceed this level? If our students only achieve minimum competency or proficiency skills, how can they compete with students around the world who achieve mastery of math, science, literate and writing skills?

What is the future of America if we fail to find ways for our students to achieve mastery of social, emotional, and cognitive standards required for a democracy? School leaders and teachers must recognize that mastery of academic knowledge, social and emotional maturity, and good character are fundamental goals for all schools.

Chapter 5

Student Engagement in the Learning Process

In September of 2008, Bob visited a preschool for three- to five-year-olds in Xian, China. His depicture of what he witnessed at the school presents important reminders for each of us regarding the true purpose of schools.

"I was one of twenty-eight educators and their spouses who arrived at this preschool that was attached to the grounds of a factory in the city of Xian. The school was composed of a two-story building designed in the shape of a large rectangle. We entered through an archway in the middle of the building that opened onto a large courtyard. The interior of the courtyard was clean and well-organized into several play and recreational areas for the children. Each classroom housed thirty students on the first and second floors of the school. There were approximately thirty classrooms. Because these preschool children were delivered to the school by their parents at 7:30 each morning, and picked up at 6:30 in the evening, small plastic cots and bedding were stacked in a section of each room so the children could nap during the day. Each classroom had tables with four chairs, cubbies to store clothing, a display center of children's storybooks, a piano, and music books in both English and Chinese. Students studied English and Chinese each day.

"They had lessons in mathematics and natural science most days, as well as civic duties. They learned to share responsibilities and treat each other with respect. They were the children of workers in the factory."

In this school, teachers modeled what they wanted children to be able to do. They dressed mostly in casual and neat clothes. In each classroom, there were two teaching assistants, and at least one person who could play the piano. Music was used frequently to initiate a lesson. Physical activities were used in the classroom and the recreational centers in the courtyard. Activities illustrated lessons and applied mathematical or natural science themes.

Frequently, as part of a game or activity, students were asked to demonstrate what they had learned.

In an English lesson that Bob observed, students were singing the song from Barney, "I Love You, You Love Me." They were asked to blow kisses to their partner and give a hug at the end of the song.

The little guy, who invited Bob to be his partner at the beginning of the song, had a strong athletic hug for him at the end of the song, which Bob returned. The teacher and students wanted Bob to lead them in a song. He asked the teacher if she knew "Old MacDonald Had a Farm." She was not sure. When he hummed a few bars, she recognized the song, at which point one of her teaching assistants went to the piano and played the song, without sheet music. Bob led the students in two verses about a cow and a duck. He had the students practice a "moo" like a cow while walking in a circle. Then, they practiced a "quack" like a duck and modeled the duck's waddle as they walked in a circle. The teacher had the class follow her as she imitated Bob's antics. She and the students sang the two verses of the song. After one practice, all of the children joined Bob in the song. They did it together twice with the teacher as Bob led the way. Then, accompanied by the piano, the teacher, leading the way, had the students sing and act out the song. She was very pleased to demonstrate to the American educators what her children had learned.

Later, when the American educators visited with the teacher, she noted that there were few male preschool teachers. She stated her belief that the students needed to see more male teachers in the schools. She was very enthusiastic about her children and their ability to cooperate with one another. She was proud of how well they were doing in English. It was obvious that she had children of many diverse abilities in the class, and she focused on how well each child was able to demonstrate what she wanted the class to learn.

At the end of the lesson, the teacher asked each child to shake hands with "our guests and thank them for coming to visit." Then, she modeled the behavior she wanted in the center of the room. Following her lead, each child stepped forward and put out her or his right hand to shake hands with the Americans. Children varied in their approaches from using a few English words to those who employed more complex English sentences. Bob noted that these students were four- and five-year-olds. Two variations of children's greetings illustrate the variety of English usage in the class. A tiny boy who was very shy said: "Thank you. I like you." A more robust statement came from a happy-faced young girl who said: "Thank you for visiting our class. We had fun. Please come again."

Bob believes that these were situational phrases that the children had learned before. What is impressive is how they were applying the phrases correctly in this new and unique situation as their teacher stepped back, out of the way, to let them perform on their own. She took great pride in the fact that every child tried to make a personal statement of "goodbye," and that all of the children were successful in this effort.

In many American classrooms, teachers model new behaviors and motivate children to imitate them. These same teachers often engage children in learning processes using manipulative objects for math or science. They employ a variety of poems, songs, and stories to capture the imagination of their students. They accept the normal curve in achievement, and allow that some children will never achieve mastery.

When and how does the light of learning in these children wane and fade? Most parents and teachers in the United States who observe children in the elementary school will report that the engagement and enthusiasm for learning that children exhibit in the preschool and primary grades begins to decline at third or fourth grade. When extensive academic testing and drill and practice for exams begin to intensify, student enthusiasm for learning and their natural curiosity wane.

Ken Bossert (2008) investigated primary and intermediate teachers in several schools on Long Island, New York, where all of the teachers had been trained in the effective teaching methods proposed by Danielson (1996). He reported that teachers in the intermediate grades differed significantly in their use of creative activities. In the primary grades, teachers focused on activities to promote learning and apply knowledge.

Bossert found that intermediate grade teachers, even after extensive training in effective teaching practices, were less likely to use creative activities in class, and were more likely to spend extensive parts of weekly lessons on drill and practice. They were worried that their students would not do well on state exams. Many other researchers report similar findings (Marzano, Pickering and Pollock, 2001).

Why are we doing all of this testing? Is it to raise standards and academic achievement among students in the United States? What a foolish endeavor. Dr. Edwards Deming (1994), the guru of quality in manufacturing, service industries, and education, noted that one cannot test excellence into a system. Excellence is the outcome of excellent systems. Systems have to be designed to produce excellence, quality minds capable of reasoning, of curiosity and discovery, of creativity, and of service to others.

Life-long learners and citizens who engage in creative problem solving are not developed by testing systems. Students who are dedicated to learning, practicing, exploring, and discovery are developed by teachers who inspire them. They learn to ask important questions, seek answers, and justify what they believe to be true. Students have to practice what they wish to master (Gladwell, 2008).

Students who write well have teachers who communicate well. Their teachers model a love of language, and engage students in ways that help them to take joy in the use of words. Students and teachers celebrate sentences that are well-crafted with cherished meanings in effective writing workshops (Graves, 1990). What standardized tests measure these disciplines and virtues?

Schools that work for students engage them in the life of the school, in the lives of their peers, their neighbors, and their community. It does not matter if a child is born in a city to poor parents or in a rural or suburban community, poverty is a barrier to academic, social, or professional achievement (Payne, 1998). Schools are the only means that society has to break a cycle of poverty within a family.

Democracies cannot survive for long with a growing underclass that cannot find work. Students have to learn how to seek renewal in a constantly changing economy and understand how to apply civic virtues to social demands. We have witnessed schools that change the lives of poor, middle-class, and wealthy children of every race, gender, and religion. We need more of these schools.

In schools where students become life-long learners, the faculty adheres to the basic beliefs that Benjamin Bloom (1981) espoused in *All Our Children Learning* where he offered a system to ensure that all children would learn. He presented five components of a unified system:

1. Stimulate children to perceive aspects of the world about them, and to fix these aspects in the child's memory by the use of language.
2. Develop more extended and accurate language. The child's comments must be extended by teacher responses. The interaction between the teacher and the child and among children should lead to more precision, complexity, and variety in the use of language.
3. Develop a sense of mastery over aspects of the immediate environment and an enthusiasm to learn for its own sake. The primary goal is to learn how to learn, to explore, and to interpret increasingly complex environments.
4. Develop thinking and reasoning and the ability to make new discoveries for oneself. Problems should be presented in the forms of games and play so that children can figure out and solve their own problems.
5. Develop purposive learning activity and the ability to attend to issues for longer periods of time. Encourage the child with feedback and reinforcement as she or he engages in various activities, and solves problems successfully. (Adapted from pp. 82–83)

Where does one find short-answer tests and teaching to a test in Bloom's Taxonomy of Cognitive operations? Grant Wiggins and Jay McTighe reduced Bloom's more complex domains of cognition, psychomotor, and affective skills to six basic elements that effective teachers should address. In their book, *Understanding by Design*, Wiggins and McTighe (2005) propose six facets of understanding: explanation, interpretation, application, perspective, empathy, and self-knowledge (pp. 76–77).

They ask that curriculum design attend to how instruction will enable students to explain what they learn, and to interpret an event. They expect that students who interpret events or phenomena will analyze the meaningful connections and significance within events.

In the Wiggins and McTighe system, when students apply knowledge, they adjust understandings to diverse, complex and difficult contexts. Students demonstrate personal perspective by effectively critiquing other viewpoints. When they offer a penetrating or novel assessment of events, they express perspective, empathy, and self-knowledge.

Instruction that fails to help students to achieve empathy, so that they are disposed and able to see and feel as others do, defaults on the very basic tenets of education. Empathetic education opens students to diverse and even unusual people and events and fosters tolerance, not conversions.

Wiggins and McTighe pose the challenge that instruction should lead students to become deeply aware of the boundaries of their own and others' understanding. Education should help students clarify their own sense of integrity and courage. They should face how they prejudge and engage in projections about other people, places, historical events, and topical issues. They should examine their convictions and their doubts.

Do our standardized tests measure these virtues? They do not. If we instruct our students beyond the narrow curricula measured in standardized tests, most of our students will perform competently on any test. If we teach to these standardized tests, think of all we will have abandoned in our culture and in our children's future. Are not eight years of a failed system of testing enough to show that we have misspent millions of dollars testing our children?

Since 2000, we should have been developing a better school system in which teachers could work. We have another chance in 2009. When Barack H. Obama, in his inaugural address as President of the United States, called for America to return to its tried and true virtues of "honesty and hard work, courage and fair play, tolerance and curiosity, and loyalty and patriotism" (Obama, 2009), he was calling for America's schools to return to their original mission of developing just citizens for a democracy.

Citizens who take responsibility for themselves, "who embody a spirit of service and who are willing to find meaning in something greater than themselves," (Obama, 2009) come from children raised in schools and homes where there is an ethos of care.

Children who feel they belong to their school, who believe their teachers care about them and who are engaged in learning under the guidance of a highly qualified teacher, become productive citizens.

Testing systems and standardized tests address none of these issues. Spending large portions of the school year preparing students to take high-stakes exams waste the time and energy of many fine educators. Testing children in grades three to eight does little to improve schools. Sadly, as a nation, our focus on test scores leads us astray from our main mission, that is to guide the development of productive adults for a democratic society.

A few schools have found ways to ignore the effects of testing by establishing a greater mission. They relegate the state testing system to a more basic and rudimentary function similar to garbage collecting where the routine of collecting garbage occurs on a planned and scheduled basis in a manner that does not disrupt the normal flow of life in a community. Standardized testing procedures should operate similarly in our school systems. Data should be collected unobtrusively and not disturb the important learning processes of the school. Standardized testing should be a group x-ray that offers an academic health card for each individual in the group. Tests do not prescribe and do not interpret interventions, effective teachers and school leaders do.

In the schools where students were highly engaged in learning, teachers were encouraged to more profoundly describe the curricula. They designed student assessment systems. They celebrated learning and their students' capacity to apply their learning to the larger world. Principals who could assess teaching and learning led these schools. They did not rely on testing systems to improve the schools. Quality teaching and learning were daily activities that these school leaders encouraged and rewarded.

At some of the best schools, average children in the primary grades operate their own learning teams at computer stations. We observed teachers train students in cooperative learning processes (Johnson and Johnson, 2005; Slavin, 1989) where each student on a team had a particular responsibility for the team's final product. We saw students rotate leadership roles on these teams.

In true cooperative-learning schools, all teachers held students collectively and individually responsible to demonstrate mastery of what they had learned. Students could apply what they knew in diverse situations. They devised their own learning within complex phenomena by writing and interpreting what a snail did to find food in a virtual aquarium.

In these effective schools, once teachers had a common understanding of the larger purpose of the curricula, they were given time to collaborate within the school day. Their creative and curious personalities took over. They developed unique and engaging lessons where students worked hard to acquire new knowledge.

Sadly, these schools seem to be the exception in America, as standardized testing drives so much of the work of schools in the beginning of the 21st century. America has an opportunity in 2009, with a new President and First Lady who have elementary-aged children, to provide for the public schools the same environment that Mr. and Mrs. Obama's children will experience in their safe, private school.

Early in his career, Bob taught in a safe, private school in Westchester County, New York. He learned what wealthy parents did for their children to support them at school. He learned that every child was expected to do well. Teachers and administrators adjusted school efforts and personnel to the learning needs of the child.

The school did not adjust the curriculum down or lower expectations. The school did not isolate the child. Teachers responded to the child and found ways to help the child learn. The child would receive the time, the attention, and the support necessary to learn what the challenging curriculum required. One-on-one tutoring would be done in an appropriate way.

In tutoring sessions, teachers were trained to listen to the child's explanations. By listening, teachers learned what barriers to new knowledge the child had. The teacher and child were expected to work together to discover new pathways to the knowledge application the task required. They were expected to seek mastery skills in all subjects.

How did this happen? Parents demanded this methodology. School leaders were hired to implement this child-centered learning community. Teachers were trained to deliver this learning process. Teachers recognized student strengths and weaknesses in tutorial sessions and used this knowledge of the child to adjust instruction in the regular classroom. Learning and mastery knowledge were the only guiding principles for teaching in this exclusive setting.

In another setting, Bob dealt with a middle-school child who exhibited an emotional and cognitive barrier to Spanish Language processes. His father told Bob that his son could not pass the subject. Bob asked the father what the child liked. The father said: "Sports of any kind." When Bob met the boy, he asked him what he would most like to do with his friends. The boy said: "Play football." "Do you have one?" Bob asked. He said he did. Bob told him: "Get it and let's go outside." They tossed the ball for a few minutes and then Bob started speaking Spanish to him and directing him to throw the ball to him at various spots and speeds.

Then, Bob asked him to call out commands to him in Spanish. They tossed the football and shared commands in Spanish a couple of days each week before every tutorial. During a period of five weeks, the boy mastered most of the common verb forms and sentence structures he would encounter in his

Spanish classes. He became confident of his academic skills. He improved his throwing arm and graduated high school with a fine average.

Every child has some strength, some interest that a teacher can employ to break barriers to new learning.

At that safe and challenging elementary school Bob had visited in Westchester County there were multiple opportunities for students to take on leadership roles. Some of the students with the best averages and some with mediocre averages held leadership positions in the primary, intermediate and seventh and eighth grades.

Every student was in a homeroom, and each homeroom had class officers. There were student papers, a literary magazine, drama society, band, chorus, orchestra, student government, social action, and service clubs. Intramural sport teams operated at every grade level as well as interscholastic competitions in sports and spelling, debate, and chess.

Any public elementary school could be structured to reproduce the best environment that the private elite schools offer. If the public school leaders believed that the children were worthy of the very best learning opportunities, they would provide them.

City school districts with high dropout rates need Kindergarten to Grade Eight community schools so that youthful leaders can be developed at school. Pre-kindergarten to third-grade classes should be no larger than fifteen students. Fourth- to eighth-grade students should have classes no larger than twenty-four students. All students in the intermediate grades should have responsibilities at school.

City school leaders have to change the size, structure, beliefs, practices, and relationships among children and adults in our public schools. They must begin with new structures that are bound tightly to the best opportunities and agents in their neighborhoods.

Sadly, many school leaders, teachers, and policy makers believe only the elite deserve the very best education, and the rest of our children have deficits that they cannot overcome.

Interestingly, the cost of restructuring a school for the success of all children would be less than the cost of drill and practice test preparation sessions and constant remediation programs that alienate our children and drive them further from becoming life-long learners.

In the elementary schools, the simplest form of student leadership is exercised by students whose teachers incorporate cooperative learning practices within their classrooms (Johnson and Johnson, 2005; Slavin, 1989). Cooperative learning is a pedagogical practice in which students have assigned roles within a small learning group of two or four students. Each group has an appropriate assignment with a clear purpose and a defined assessment system. Students know that they will be assessed individually as well as collectively.

In cooperative learning endeavors, students produce a group product and demonstrate individual mastery of the major body of knowledge. Their teachers provide individual assessments of mastery within the task. Individual external assessments are used too such as written essays, research papers or portfolios, PowerPoint presentations, and debates.

Some days, students deliver mini-lectures to the class. Newsletters written by the students with bylines attached to each author's work, as well as news shows and video clips, comprise some of the operational work that students do to demonstrate what they know and can do.

Leadership roles for students within each cooperative group change monthly and students learn to work together, to respect one another, to fulfill individual responsibilities, and to support the group's efforts. Many multicultural schools employ cooperative learning techniques as part of weekly lessons, and report more peaceful relations among students as a result of these efforts (Johnson and Johnson, 2005; Slavin, 1989).

Effective schools train new teachers and students how to use cooperative learning techniques annually. Cooperative learning is part of the school landscape. Students who travail across this landscape motivate each other to succeed and to excel. Cooperative learning processes are part of every student's experience in class.

In band, the woodwinds, the percussion, and the brass sections have cooperative learning events every week. Successful teachers orchestrate the learning processes, motivate and elicit the best performances from their students. Cooperative learning is one of their basic techniques. They use it to draw together diverse students in a common mission that involves the acquisition of skills to perform a musical composition.

Middle schools and high schools face particularly difficult challenges as students become more and more independent in their learning modes and their preferred communicative styles on the Internet. Teachers and administrators need to know how the Internet is used at their school among their students. Part of the new obligations that educators must accept is teaching appropriate etiquette, protocols, and techniques as well as safe and fair use of the Internet (Ihne, 2009).

Rather than try to police a technology that defies monitoring, school leaders and teachers should focus on instilling in their students the values and beliefs that would ensure a wise use of the Internet. In her study of middle school students, Ihne (2009) found that personal integrity predicted less cyberbullying among boys and girls in eighth grade. Also, she found that even in schools that claimed to have teachers trained in cooperative learning and students trained in peer mediation, neither strategy was pervasive and part of everyone's experience.

Goodenow (1992) and Finn and Voelkl (1993) reported that a sense of belonging at school, acceptance by teachers and peers, and engagement in learning and school activities were factors related to academic achievement for Black, White, and Hispanic students. In a school, these important interpersonal factors did not evolve by accident. They were planned, developed, and nurtured annually by school leaders.

Deci and Ryan (2000) examined the factors that contributed to student academic achievement. They found student need for self-determination in the process of learning and clear goals were related to higher levels of academic achievement.

Connell, Spencer and Aber (1994) noted that intervention strategies were necessary to positively influence student and parent engagement in school. Students and parents had to learn how to engage in school activities, and how to support one another and the teachers. Sirin (2004) associated positive student and parent relationships with higher levels of student engagement in school.

In his study of sixth grade students, Grimaldi (2009) found that student engagement in lessons was directly related to the quality of interactions that teachers had with students. Black males in his study responded positively to increases in teacher responses to their questions in mathematics class, and outperformed similar peers in less responsive classrooms.

What better way to engage parents and students could there be than to use the Internet as a cooperative learning experience for classmates and parents? Think of the many and varied virtual events that teachers and their students could devise to incorporate the knowledge and experience of parents into a research project. Instead of science fairs that parents have to leave work to attend, they could participate in virtual science research activities with their children. They could explore a myth, a historical event, or scientific discovery. Using our resources to collaborate with teams of parents and students could add productivity to many cooperative learning events.

Furrer and Skinner (2003) found that students who related positively to parents, teachers, and peers were more engaged in school activities. Wilson (2004) surveyed students in nine middle schools and ten high schools and found that students who felt connected to their schools experienced lower levels of aggression.

McNeely and Falci (2004) cautioned that although students who form attachments to their teachers tend to have more positive social behaviors, their attachments to peers influence their behaviors positively or negatively depending on the values of the peer group.

Generally, students who felt closer to their teachers believed that their teachers cared about them as individuals, and these students expressed higher levels of school engagement and demonstrated higher academic achievement (Gest, Welsh and Dometrovich, 2005).

In a study of black high school gang and non-gang members, Humphrey (2008) cautioned educators not to be "patsies," and to hold all students to high standards of ethical, courteous, and academic conduct. Caring educators were an essential part of the landscape of school effectiveness as long as the caring attitudes were matched with high expectations for all students.

In an analysis of a highly successful discipline code at a moderate wealth-high tax school district in Long Island, Bob interviewed the assistant principal, James Lynch, who explained that the district and the high school discipline codes were developed in cooperation with a quality planning team of parents, students, teachers, and administrators.

One of the most critical values that the team discussed early in its deliberations was how to communicate to students that the code was there to help them be successful and not to exclude them from school. As part of their team discussions, members determined that a "zero-tolerance" policy for school failure or discipline that excluded students from after-school activities like sports or musicals would not be effective. Zero tolerance might even be destructive to the larger mission of the school.

They established a guiding idea that in all applications of discipline, the school officials would seek ways to encourage better behavior and more success among students.

In order to provide more options for educators to motivate students to learn, they wanted to encourage appropriate behavior and reduce inappropriate behavior. The quality planning team members looked for ways to continue a student's education and to promote better behavior at the same time.

One ingenious method they selected revolved around a discussion of eligibility for athletic interscholastic competitions. Rather than exclude a student for one or more failures in a class subject, they decided that as long as the student attended after-school tutorials weekly and showed progress in the tutorial setting with a teacher, the student who had failed a subject could remain eligible for interscholastic sports.

Quality planning teams in West Babylon, New York, operated as quality circles in which members reflected on the benefits of a policy and suggested a variety of responses. Quality circle members selected the best option that would serve the mission of the district. In this case, the quality circle decided that all co-curricular activities should require the same eligibility as the sports program. Therefore, in West Babylon High School, to be eligible for extra and co-curricular activities students would have to demonstrate successful class performance or progress in after-school tutorials in the subject in which they had poor test performance.

Teachers were given the power to manage student eligibility, and students had the power to control their own eligibility through sincere efforts to learn.

As the quality planning team managed by Assistant Principal, James Lynch, examined the new policy in relationship to current practices and structures at West Babylon High School, they realized they had to make some necessary structural changes to the daily school schedule. They proposed that all after-school activities begin fifty minutes after the school day ended so that students in need of tutorials could attend them without missing the beginning of their co-curricular practice sessions. For students waiting to begin after-school activities, the large cafeterias, the school library, and large lecture halls were reopened for study halls, supervised by staff members who received a stipend for that work.

Advisors to clubs and other activities were permitted to open their supervised locales to study hall students at the end of the school day as long as the faculty advisor was there to supervise.

Essentially, the whole school became populated with multi-grade study halls at the end of every day. Faculty advisors and upperclassmen helped students complete their essential homework in study halls and co-curricula learning sessions.

After five years of continuous improvement, 92 percent of the high school students were engaged at least one day each week in a school club, activity, music or theatre performing group. Art, technology, science and math clubs, newspaper, the literary magazine, the Yearbook, and sports-related programs flourished. The middle school operated under the same guidelines, and had similar levels of participation.

Each year, in the spring before incoming students came to their new secondary schools in Lynch's district, they were met by senior students at the school activity fair and invited to join a club, performing arts group, theatre group, service group, or athletic team. Senior students explained and demonstrated what their preferred activity did. They invited prospective first-year students to sign up for further contacts the first week of school.

Guidance counselors reviewed the names of those who signed up for an activity, and called students who did not sign up and their parents. They encouraged students to participate in some activity. The principals had an assistant principal in each school assigned to monitor student participation in class and in extra- and co-curricular activities.

When the initial plan to engage students in school activities began, only 34 percent of the student population grades nine through twelve was engaged in extra- or co-curricular activities. Because student involvement in activities and sports had become part of the quality monitoring process, teachers and administrators were able to remove activities that had few participants. Instead of high-cost and low-quality school activities, this school system listened to its students, deleted what did not work and instituted programs for students that responded to their interests and high expectations.

In the place of poorly attended activities, new activities were designed by faculty, students, and parents that elicited higher enthusiasm among students. Parents were a large part of the solutions to student motivation at school because they responded also to the interests and personal aspirations of their children as volunteers and enthusiastic providers of the extra help that the school needed.

When student participation reached 90 percent, vandalism costs dropped significantly in both schools. The funds that had been spent previously on repairs at the schools were redirected to the activity funds for students. Students were made aware of the fact that much of the financial support that they enjoyed came from funds that were previously spent on the repair of facilities. As this word spread, vandalism declined further.

James Lynch summed up his view of the co-curricular program with this statement: "Our students were learning to give back to the community, learning to lead and to develop skills that they would need as adults. Our quality team meets every four years to review all aspects of the program, including the disciplinary code. In fact, in 2009, we have all aspects of the extra- and co-curricular programs under review."

Schools that have engaged students in the learning process have not been lucky. They have been led by committed educators who want to see all children learn and enjoy enriched stimulating, learning environments. Such schools have school leaders who believe in the collective wisdom of the faculty, the parents, and the students. They manage the school with collaborative, quality teams whose goals are to improve teaching and learning in a continuous process.

Effective school leaders set high expectations for everyone including themselves. They hold each person responsible for his and her share in the achievements of the school. These leaders have a clear mission, methodology, and criteria for success. Everyone knows what they expect. In these effective schools, published curricula are available for anyone to examine and critique. Supervision of instruction and learning is collaborative, exploratory, and conducive to constant improvement.

In effective schools, students are engaged in the life of the school because the climate, the values and the philosophy of everyone attached to the school demands such commitment. Students enjoy the challenges they encounter inside and outside of the classroom and the triumphs of a job well done at these schools. They interact with many other students and involve themselves in the life of their community. They engage in learning activities as part of a larger design.

The classroom is structured to engage students in a variety of cooperative learning endeavors. Outside the classroom, the school is organized in ways that promote and support student involvement in a variety of extra- and co-curricular activities. Schools that work for students have systems that work for students too.

Every school leader should have a quality team of students, parents, faculty and staff that examines the quality of student engagement in the life of the school. The level of commitment students make to learning and co-curricular activities should be examined annually. The potential growth of many and varied activities that expand student commitment to learning and service to others should be part of the quality team agenda, monthly. Students always should have a forum for consideration of their ideas in effective schools.

Such schools work for students, and in the long run, for parents, teachers, staff, and our society. In the Sunday edition of the New York Times of February 8, 2009, Richard Nisbett, Professor of Psychology at the University of Michigan, wrote of the successes of the Perry Preschool in Ypsilanti, Michigan, in the early 1960s where highly trained and motivated teachers worked daily with groups of six preschoolers to help the children develop cognitively and socially.

They visited the children and their families for ninety minutes each week and "By the time these students reached high school, almost half of them scored above the tenth percentile on the California Achievement Test compared with only 14 percent in a control group" (Week in Review, p. 12).

Nesbitt offers the KIPP Schools (Knowledge is Power Program) of San Francisco as another example of effective schools serving minority children in middle schools. Knowledge is Power Program schools open at 7:30 a.m., and engage their young students in a variety of classes, learning activities, and co-curricular programs until 5:00 p.m., daily. Uniquely, for California schools after Proposition 13, in which local taxes were restricted from rising more than 2.5 percent annually, the KIPP students enjoy sports, art, music, theatre, dance, photography, and visits to museums. After one year, student performance on the Stanford Achievement Test math rose from 37 percent at or above the national average to 65 percent (New York Times, Week in Review, p. 12).

Nesbitt notes that school culture makes a difference. The culture of the school is highly dependent on the beliefs of the school leader and the teachers. Where school leaders view students as children with deficits, they allow remediation and social ills to account for student failures. Teachers in these schools spend most of their instructional time diagnosing deficiencies and seeking specialists to treat their students.

We find that school faculties that have a cultural belief that their students are deficient in a variety of social skills, knowledge, courtesies, and motivations, also hold low expectations for their students. They spend inordinate amounts of time testing students, classifying students, and assigning blame for student failure to home failures. Generally, they avoid the hard work of teaching and learning that the children really need.

Schools that employ leaders and teachers who view students as unique people with a variety of interests and talents motivate them to explore knowledge and solve problems. These teachers work together with their students. They see their students as people who come to school with toolboxes stuffed with things that can be used to promote learning (Page, 2008). Each child has a unique toolbox. Teachers use the child's toolbox to guide a child in the discovery of scientific truths, and historical and social events. Their students engage in a multiplicity of differentiated learning. Events and unusual questions stimulate these students to master basic academic skills. Their teachers encourage them to use their cognitive and psychological talents to tackle complex and engrossing questions.

We witnessed the effects of a middle-school science teacher in a highly diverse small city school system. One day each week, the teacher presented a scientific myth to the students and asked them to solve it within seven days. Every seventh day was discovery day. All the other days were dedicated to learning the scientific methods and practices that the students would need to solve the next riddle or myth they were to encounter. Every child in the class was engaged in scientific discovery. Every child in the class knew how to work in a cooperative group.

It is not the province of special schools like the Perry Preschool or the KIPP middle school to engage students in learning. A school does not have to be special to work for children. School leaders and teachers have to first believe that all children can learn. Secondly, teachers must believe that they can make the difference in their students' learning cycle. Thirdly, teachers must engage the children in real and live learning events that have been well thought out. Teachers who think of themselves as professionals, who avoid seeing their students as deficit individuals, who look for the toolbox each child brings to school, find ways to teach all children.

Cooperative learning, planned and well-structured leadership opportunities for students, curricula focused on student performance, and learned applications of knowledge are systems that require the best thinking from students and teachers.

Team learning and quality circles for teachers can guide the discovery of many effective instructional practices. When teachers work in cooperative learning teams, they select more appropriate and inventive interventions. They pose creative and unique questions to students. They find interventions that help students learn.

School leaders who are well-versed in the active development of teachers and students are committed to the full involvement of parents in the learning cycle of the school. They know that parents comprise a major force for change in school systems that work for students. Headmasters and principals of the finest schools have incorporated the strengths of their parents into their school designs for many decades. When leaders believe children are worthy of the best and parents insist on the best for their children, schools deliver.

What President Barack Obama and First Lady Michelle Obama can do for the public schools of Washington, D. C., and Chicago and the rest of the nation is demand that they offer the same enriched environment that their own children's private school offers. The Obama children are not going to be tested in a high-stakes environment annually. They will not be subjected to test preparation, and drill and practice for math and language tests exclusive of creative instruction. They will enjoy the creative and supportive learning environment that John Dewey promulgated a century ago.

They will receive an enriched and creative learning curricula designed to engage their minds and spirits. They will receive an education. We want all children to have the same opportunity. Forget the constant grade-level tests and the high cost of this testing system that fails to produce benefits for the nation or the child. Spend the money on learning.

Rewards make a difference. Reward schools for growth in learning that students demonstrate. Use Local Chapters of National Associations of the Arts, Music, mathematics, science, history, and language arts to adjudicate student performance at regional competitions. Give schools federal grants in aid of $5,000 for every student who scores a grade of excellent on a creative or subject competition. For students who earn a four or five on a national Advanced Placement test, award $10,000 of federal grant money to the schools for targeted purposes that add technology to the classroom, promote teacher professional development, and reward the residents and businesses for the success of the children with tax reductions. Reward success and see how many more successful students that school develops.

The old system of testing excellence into schools has not worked, and never will work. If President Obama wants change in America's public schools, then his administration and Congress should reward excellence. If excellence is rewarded in schools, the nation will find excellence expanding in its schools (Stone, 1997).

Chapter 6

How to Govern Schools Effectively

Thomas Friedman in his book *The World is Flat* (2006), wrote: "The first, and most important, ability you can develop in a flat world is the ability to 'learn how to learn'—to constantly absorb, and teach yourself, new ways of doing old things or new ways of doing new things" (p. 302).

School boards in the United States are under a great deal of public pressure to reduce the cost of schooling, to expand the financial base of the schools, and to improve the academic achievement and the quality of teaching in the schools. Many school board members report that their boards do not have a clear understanding of their role and responsibilities.

Chait, Holland, and Taylor (1996) conclude: "effective governance by a board of trustees is a relatively rare and unnatural act" (p. 1). They believe that boards tend to simply drift with the tide, indicating that no set priorities are established for their governing processes.

"The challenges of raising student achievement in the 21st century suggest a more meaningful and dynamic governance role for local school boards in setting education policy—that of providing leadership to school systems as they establish and strive for high levels of student performance" (Resnick, 1999, p. 1).

Smoley (1999) observed: "New school board members focus on the specific issues that brought them to office" (p. 12). They distrust the superintendent, and believe a variety of complaints from the community. Their lack of trust leads to a focus on details and management issues. Smoley reports that conflicting issues and unrelated minor initiatives grab the attention of board members, misdirect them and encourage them to operate without a pattern or plan.

Carver (2000) noted: "School governance is fraught with the ironic combination of micromanagement and rubber-stamping, as well as an array of tradition-blessed practices that trivialize the board's important public policy role" (p. 1). He created a model of school governance, known as Policy Governance. "The model requires as much discipline as boards require of staffs, calls upon boards to be strategic and visionary leaders and imposes a set of carefully crafted principles to distinguish board decisions from managerial and professional ones" (Carver, 2000, p. 2).

According to Carver, school boards should exercise their authority by identifying the parameters within which the superintendent may act and the acceptable standards for employee behavior. They set goals and hold the superintendent, as chief executive, responsible to meet the defined expectations of the board.

In Carver's governance model, the superintendent is responsible for the adherence to the vision, mission, and district goals that the staff and the students exhibit. Carver's model assumes that a highly optimistic set of professional skills and attitudes exist among board members.

He assumes that if boards lack these skills, they are willing to be trained to operate within these sophisticated guidelines. Many board members report that they are not interested in board training (Chait, Holland, and Taylor, 1996; Turnow, 2002; Mauro, 2006).

Individual board members often find it difficult to make the transition from managerial work, where they have responsibilities to do something individually, to the role demands of a governance body, because the structure of a board is not individual.

A school board is a collective body whose members act as one agent on behalf of the community, its employees, and, of course, its mission and the students it serves. In the case of schools, students and, more specifically, many young children must be part of the primary focus of the school board. It is not a small task to serve the interests of a large community, and to balance the needs for educational funds with the financial resources available to a community.

Carver (1997) described the unique governance challenges of a school board using structural and interpersonal terms. He wrote:

> Boards are at the extreme end of the accountability chain. Other managers must deal with persons both above and below their stations. The buck stops with the board. It has no supervisor to carve out what portion of a given topic it is to oversee.
>
> The board acts, in a moral sense and sometimes a legal one, as agent of a largely unseen and often undecided principal, an entity that expresses itself in curious ways, if at all.
>
> The board is a set of individuals operating as a single entity. Melding multiple peer viewpoints and values into a single resolution is peculiar to a group acting collectively as a manager.

Individuals' discipline tends to suffer when they belong to groups.

A board is likely to have less discipline than any one of its members operating alone.

Boards are ordinarily more than the usual managerial arm's length from the next lower organizational level. They are not only part-time, but also physically removed (p. 16).

School boards need to recognize the limits on their powers and, at the same time, understand how to apply their collective wisdom to the development of their school system. Goodman and Zimmerman (2000) expressed an optimistic view of school boards: "For our part, we remain undismayed by the critics' incessant chant that the system is broken and must be rebuilt. Rather than lament public education's shortcomings, we prefer to build on its achievements . . ." (p. 2). There is much wisdom in what they note. Districts have strengths. They have large toolboxes at each school filled with stuff to help students learn. Boards have to learn how to motivate school leaders, faculty, and staff to maximize their strengths and initiate the change required to have all students master the school curricula.

Smoley (1999) provided statements to help boards assess their own behaviors. There is little research about the data that inform boards about their effectiveness. Because of the lack of research on how school boards operated, in 1999 Dowling College began to investigate a continuum of behaviors that might provide a framework for effective boards.

Previously, Baldwin and Hughes (1995) attempted to describe four characteristics of effective governance that private school trustees seemed to employ for their schools: visionary leadership, setting of organizational parameters, establishing personnel policies for hiring, continuance, compensation, and general management of strategic plans.

Chait, Holland, and Taylor (1996) were interested in effective college boards. They visited twenty-two college campuses to interview and survey trustees and presidents in the Trustee Demonstration Project. They divided the competencies of effective boards into six dimensions: contextual, educational, interpersonal, analytical, political, and strategic.

Hughes, Manley, and Rudiger (2001) examined private and public school trustee responses to questions about their practices, and noted that their responses could be grouped into four governance practices: professional leadership, policy guidance, structured decision-making efforts and general management endeavors in finance, personnel development, and compensation issues.

Ruck (2003) used the work of Chait, Holland, and Taylor with college boards to develop a scale to measure school board effectiveness and its relationship to several governance practices. He employed many of the concepts that Chait et al. identified in their educational dimension for his descriptions of effective boards. Ruck's measurement of board effectiveness examined how the board discussed its own performance, sought community input, offered orientation for new members, received feedback, and explicitly evaluated its own responsibilities.

Turnow (2003) examined conflict among board members, and noted that board members in her study tended to describe conflict between members as low. Where conflict did exist, the board members saw it as negatively related to board effectiveness. Hawkins (2003) investigated team learning and governance practices and found that his measurement of team learning was highly related to board effectiveness. Feltman (2003) investigated coercive practices among school board members, and found that 25 percent of the board members reported that they had been victims of a coercive practice initiated by another board member. The board's ability to learn as a team emerged as a critical factor in board effectiveness.

Grucci (2004) used many of the constructs developed by Hughes, Manley, and Rudiger (2000), Ruck (2002), and Hawkins (2003) to investigate relationships of financial forecasting and financial management to board effectiveness. She found that financial practices were highly related to the boards' sense of effectiveness. Eisenberg (2005) analyzed financial practices, governance issues, and board effectiveness among school board trustees who attended the state convention for the New York State School Board Association in October of 2003. Among those New York State school board members, she found teamwork to be the dimension that predicted the largest amount of effectiveness among the boards.

Carr (2004) explored the governance competencies identified by the National School Board Association in 2000. He surveyed New York State school board members from rural, suburban, and small-city school districts regarding: vision development, setting standards for student achievement, assessment programs, accountability programs, resource alignment for achievement, district climate, collaboration, and continuous improvement. He found that school boards that aligned an overall statement of vision and goals and standards for student achievement experienced high levels of effectiveness.

Mauro (2006), in a study of school board members who served in a variety of low- and high-wealth districts within the suburbs of Long Island, found that governance practices that included openness to board development were related to a high sense of board effectiveness.

Burak (2006), in a study of urban and suburban school districts in the northeast of the United States, investigated the relationship of school-board curriculum evaluation practices to board effectiveness. She was one of the first researchers to connect student achievement and school board practices in curriculum evaluation to board effectiveness. She found that professional leadership, teamwork, and curriculum evaluation practices of the boards were highly related to board members' effectiveness. In addition, she noted that boards that exhibited appropriate financial management and planning practices as well as attention to policy issues had the foundational skills to be effective.

DIMENSIONS OF GOVERNANCE

Boards that cannot achieve a sense of professionalism in their daily inter-actions have difficulty being effective as a governing body. Professional leadership is the extent to which the school board has respectful commu-nications with the superintendent, and members exhibit respect for each other. Their focus on the school district's mission, goals, and regard for community values is highly related to their sense of effectiveness (Feltman, 2003).

There are many ways to examine how boards of education operate. We want to provide a practical and user-friendly way for superintendents and school board members to evaluate how they are operating. The most effec-tive boards view the superintendent as a non-voting member of the board, one who serves as the chief advisor to the board and who shares the concerns, vision, and mission of the board.

Effective boards establish a partnership with the superintendent, and accept the superintendent as the chief executive for the school district. At the same time, the board members maintain owners' rights and duties to evaluate the chief executive.

After many years of research with school boards in the New York region, we examined board practices in a large national study led by Judith Chen (2008). Chen found that school finance and financial management and plan-ning skills were the highest concern among school board members across the nation. In 2009, after the largest recession and the greatest drop in housing values in fifty years in the US, school finance remains a major concern of all school board members.

Without the large amount of funding for public schools from President Obama's 2009 federal aid package to the states, teacher layoffs would have been rampant across the United States. We believe that school board mem-bers need to focus on a few practices that comprise their governing duties and responsibilities if they are to be effective.

First, they should have a method to evaluate their own professional practice. We suggest they monitor the following behaviors:

1. Ensure respectful communications with the superintendent.
2. Respect each other.
3. Trust in the good intentions of peers.
4. Enjoy working together.
5. Know authority rests with the whole board.

Another essential element that effective boards understand and monitor, is the policy leadership of the board. Carver (2000) stressed that board members had to learn how to attend to the ends or desired results that the board sought. They had to permit administrators the autonomy to develop and implement the means to the ends within the parameters set by the board.

Carver proposed six understandings that effective boards should adopt:

1. Governance is seen as a specialized form of ownership rather than a specialized form of management.
2. The board as a body is vested with governing authority so that measures that preclude trustees from exercising individual authority are crucial to governance integrity.
3. The board, on behalf of the public, specifies the nature and cost of consumer results.
4. The board outlines boundaries, within which the superintendent and staff are permitted free choice of means.
5. The board monitors performance on ends and unacceptable means in systematic and rigorous way.
6. Board meetings are spent largely in learning about, debating, and resolving long-term ends rather than dealing with otherwise delegable matters (p. 8).

We believe that effective boards have a clear orientation towards policy management, and conduct their governance efforts in very specific ways. They use policy to evaluate hiring practices to set the purpose of education and to assess student achievement within the schools. They match policies to a district's mission, goals, and objectives. They establish policy for the roles of trustees and others in negotiations with employee contracts. They have policies to guide all other contractual relationships that the district may have with independent contractors and/or real estate, accounting, legal, construction, or bond advisors.

In every case, policy should be clear about the role of board members, administrators, and the method of decision making. Several ways that we like boards to assess their policy practices are listed below:

- Follow policies about the hiring of staff.
- Set policies to support the mission and objectives of the district.
- Set procedures for the development of policy.
- Set procedures for the evaluation of all policies.
- Provide policy to develop and evaluate the district's mission.
- Create policy to measure achievement of district goals.
- Set policy to guide negotiations with bargaining units.
- Set policy to guide purchases.
- Set policy to avoid conflict of interest.

The more a board attempts to direct the work of the school or to evaluate school outcomes outside of a policy management framework, the more likely the board will resort to micromanagment practices that interrupt the work of the administrators. When board members do not recognize that their authority is invested in the board as a collective body, and they exert personal pressure on employees, especially administrators, coaches, and teachers, they replace the superintendent and undermine the work of the board.

Certainly, board members are no different from other people when they take pleasure in the exercise of power. When a board member confronts individual employees in private, or exercises individual powers of persuasion outside of the board meeting and tries to control events through political pressure, the board member has become a disruptive force inside the system. Such board members have abandoned their policy role. They have chosen to operate on their own whims.

Whimsical and selfish behaviors of individual board members introduce the chaotic forces of self-interests into board decisions. Dysfunctional boards fill their agenda with personal interests and needs. Policy is designed to provide the parameters that keep a board functional, cohesive, ethical, and effective.

We would feel more confident that boards were operating as they should if board members took the time to self-reflect and evaluate how well they were guided by policy. In the deliberations and actions of the board, members should be comfortable asking how a particular action conforms to the board of education's policies.

Effective boards structure their decision-making process and their financial management practices. Boards with a structured decision-making practice publish a written plan or policy for the board's own development. They state how the Board President will advise trustees on their resposibilities.

Effective boards gather information from a variety of sources, and have a plan to analyze data before making decisions. They employ formal reports about student achievement. They are concerned with the ethnic and multicultural needs of the district. They project enrollment and clarify budgetary issues. They function openly as a corporate body.

We believe boards should look at their practices in these basic decisions annually to reflect on how well they follow planned decision-making procedures:

- Examine formal reports about student achievement.
- Consider the ethnic and multicultural needs of the district.
- Examine demographic trends in their planning.
- Assess progress towards their goals.
- Review enrollment projections to forecast budgetary needs every five years.
- Provide educational programs and training to promote board development.
- Provide authority for the board president to advise trustees on their responibilities.
- Gather information from a variety of sources for decisions and policy.
- Consider current research during the process of making decisions.
- Provide a structured method to analyze data before making curricular decisions.
- Provide a structured method to analyze data before making budgetary decisions.

Effective boards provide the leadership for the district's financial plan, and allow community input into the annual financial plan. They review alternate finance plans for capital improvements or new programs. They have a method to identify long-term costs for proposed projects before they make commitments.

Boards that lead by example establish a reflective practice for themselves and ask the right questions. We suggest that they respond to these statements of inquiry regarding their finance practice:

- Provide leadership for the financial plan of the district.
- Allow for community participation in their financial deliberations.
- Consider the tax impact on all community groups in the financial plan.
- Examine the annual budget and determine its impact on educational programs.
- Request an analysis of ongoing costs of proposed projects before committing taxpayer dollars.
- Review the financial impact of state aid projections.
- Review alternative financing plans for capital projects.

- Routinely ask questions about the treasurer's report.
- Routinely ask questions about the investment and the cash reconciliation report.
- Match revenues against planned expenditures monthly.
- Expect justification at the monthly meeting when a transfer of appropriations between codes is requested.
- Review fund-balance projections at least twice a year to anticipate modifications in the current year's spending plan.
- Compare the cost of instructional school-wide programs with regional standards for future improvements.
- Participate in cooperative bidding programs to reduce costs.

Effective boards understand their fiduciary role, and provide sufficient time to analyze and learn the intricacies of school finance. Few school board members come to the board prepared for the financial issues they will face. Therefore, it is critical that board policy and the board president and superintendent provide proper guidance to all school board members regarding their normal duties to examine financial statements.

Beyond the fiduciary duties of school board members lie a related set of duties in which board members are expected to reflect the norms of the community. In this role, it is essential that they evaluate the curriculum of the schools in terms of the school district's stated vision and mission as well as the achievements of students. Curricula should reflect the important criterion-referenced outcomes that the board adopted as part of its vision for students.

The role of the board in curriculum evaluation is not well-described in the literature on school board effectiveness. Burak (2006) tried to investigate the board's proper role in curriculum evaluation. She found that there were extensive relationships among the board's professional leadership, teamwork, effectiveness, and curriculum evaluation.

Curriculum evaluation is a vital part of the governance role of the school board. Boards often delegate their curricular responsibilities to professional educators. They fail to require that educators conduct their analysis of curriculum and its relationship to student academic performance in public session. Boards should exercise proper oversight of the curriculum by requiring that their educational leaders present curriculum evaluations in a public forum. All boards should reflect on the following statements to assess how well they are exercising their duties in curriculum evaluation:

- Evaluate literacy and the humanities curriculum in all schools.
- Evaluate math, science and technology curricula in all schools.

- Contrast curriculum programs with those of selected benchmarked districts.
- Verify that the curriculum is aligned to student needs.
- Require an analysis of student strengths and weaknesses in each curriculum.
- Publish school curricula aligned with state standards.
- Require school leaders to evaluate student academic performance.
- Require an assessment of the impact of staff development on teaching.
- Require student and teacher suveys about satisfaction with technology for instruction.

Burak (2006), in her study of northeastern school boards in the United States, discovered a critical pathway to board effectiveness that required board members to practice professional leadership, teamwork, and curriculum evaluation.

Mauro (2006), in his study of low- and high-wealth suburban school boards on Long Island, revealed that board members' openness to personal development and growth was highly related to teamwork and board effectiveness. Senge (1990) defined teamwork as the extent to which a school board exercised a common purpose, a shared vision, and an understanding of how to complement one another's efforts.

The message is very clear: effective boards operate with a professional leadership style. They have high regard for their own policy-making authority and they adhere to their policies. They require all who work or interact with the school district to do so in ways that comply with the spirit of their policies. They hold high ethical standards and do not comply with *just* the letter of the law. Such boards that know their duty provide a structured methodology to guide their actions.

They commit the time necessary to fulfill their fiduciary responsibilities and their leadership roles in curriculum evaluations. They are open to learning new skills. They seek to acquire new knowledge. They attend staff development workshops. They provide for their own training and education as board members. They model the behavior they want from others.

Where board members fail, they stop short in the final steps of a leadership process. Frequently, boards set goals and then they fail to assign authority and accontability for the goals. They stop short of setting measureable criteria that would indicate if progress had been made. They fail to provide a method to measure progress. Much of this failure is a failure of executive leadership to educate the board. In many cases, the superintendent fails to educate the staff, the board, and the community.

We recommend that boards use a simple planning tool to develop measurable goals, clear authority, and accountability. Criteria for success and methods to assess progress must be provided by the board to the superintendent, often in a collaborative process.

Table 6.1. District Planning Process for Success

Policy goal	Executive authority	Success criteria	Monitoring process
Student programs and services	Initiate a systemic examination of existing programs and services provided to students K-12		
Finance, budget and business operations	Improve the efficiency and effectiveness of the district business practices without sacrificing controls		
Bonds, construction and facility improvements	Establish capital priorities for the next five years		
School community public relations and legislative action	Engage the community in the analysis of the infrastructure		

In Table 6.1, we provide a framework for boards to use. The key to our framework is the simplicity of the planning tool. The tool has four categories. District Goals, Executive Authority, Success Criteria and Monitoring Process. Districts that monitor progess towards their avowed goals have higher success rates.

Our framework for planning, delegation, and achievement of goals assumes the board and superintendent agree to the goals. The board sets the executive authority and the parameters that limit the autonomy of the executive. The success criteria are agreed to, at the outset, by the superintendent and the board.

In cases where other subordinates of the superintendent are affected by the success criteria and its inherent accountability standards, the superintendent should be given the time he or she needs to consult with subordinates on the success criteria and the monitoring process. The monitoring process is written last as it depends on the criteria for success.

A collaborative process in a democratic society, such as the one we enjoy in the United States, produces higher commitment among employees and higher success in the long run than any autocratic system will achieve. A district Planning Process for Success includes three to five goals, executive authority, success criteria, and a monitoring process. When these areas are expicitly stated, there is little room for board members and superintendents to avoid the results. The process leads to many successes for the district, the board, the superintendent, and the staff.

Table 6.2. Board Policy Governance Expectations

Policy Area Goal	Expectation Goal	Exec Limits Delegation	Criteria for Success
Transportation	Board sets mile Limits. Board approves equipment, staff and total budget	Superintendent manages services. Superintendent controls overtime.	Parent safety score: 90 percent approval Cost per mile verified Overtime held to goal of 10 percent of budget
Finance	Board limits 5 year projection Tax increases	Superintendent manages limits	Property Tax increase below limit of 4 percent
Budget	Growth limited	Superintendent adheres to limits	Budget growth meets limits of CPI
Facilities	Board sets Improvements	Superintendent provides plans with architect	Board adopts plan Board approves construction
Grounds	Board sets Improvements	Superintendent initiates plans	Board approves funds Board satisfied
Cafeteria	Board adopts Program	Superintendent finds manager	Inspections find quality service and food
Personnel	Board approves	Superintendent recommends Superintendent evaluates	Personnel perform well or do not continue
Curriculum	Board adopts	Superintendent recommends	Criteria for student success met mastery percent
Student services	Board approves	Superintendent evaluates	Criteria for success is met
Community relations	Board plans, executes and evaluates	Superintendent consults with board & executes	Criteria for success in community is met

The board governance expectations are written around critical policy areas in which the board has important interests. Frequently, these high-interest areas require several years of continuous monitoring in order for them to establish a pattern of improvement.

Boards should not adopt more than three goals and two policy expectations at any one time. Five critical issues under review in a given year challenge the executive skills of most leaders especially when there are clear criteria for success.

Governance is a shared duty. Governing boards have a responsibility to collaborate, to be transparent in every way possible, and to accept feedback from diverse groups in the community and the district. Effective governance requires school boards to guide all of their actions by district policy. Board members must adopt a desire to serve the interests of the children. They must feel that it is their civic duty and obligation to work openly and fairly with other board members, the superintendent, and the staff.

Finally, effective governing systems operate in effective school systems. Ineffective governing systems actually prevent administrators and teachers from focusing on the main mission of the schools and, in the long run, deny many students the opportunity to fulfill their true potential.

Chapter 7

Character Education and its Impact on Student Achievement

Effective schools recognize that education includes a core set of values and civic virtues. Values and virtues construct human character and make it possible for moral beings composed of myriad impulses, such as those we experience daily, to build a democratic society.

It is not a coincidence that every society and culture has its own version of the "Golden Rule." Thomas Lickona states: "Down through history and all over the world, education has had two great goals: to help people become smart and to help them become good. 'Good' can be defined in terms of moral values that have objective worth, values that affirm our human dignity, and promote the good of the individual and society" (1991, p. 67). Ryan (2003) observed: "Socrates defined education as what we do to help young people become both smart and good" (p. 2).

Democracy relies upon citizens with good character. In the United States, test-based accountability has taken center stage in public education. The social and emotional domains, which are prerequisites to academic success, are often overlooked. Ironically, any push towards higher standards and achievement that lacks an emphasis on social and emotional literacy fails to address the maturation needs of our youth (Mental Health in Schools Program and Policy Analysis, UCLA Center, July 2006).

To meet current academic standards and expectations and the social/emotional needs of our youth, a school needs to build a learning community where students engage in a variety of developmental activities that prepare them for tomorrow's future (Darling-Hammond, 1998). Schools must develop this community realizing and celebrating its diversity. Students of diverse backgrounds need to be acculturated into our national ideals and

117

expectations for both healthy behavior and academic performance (DeLuca and Hawkins, 2007).

Lickona (1991) believes that in order for character education to be successfully implemented within our school curriculum, all constituents must agree to what good character is. Character must be broadly conceived to encompass the cognitive, affective, and behavioral aspects of morality. All adults in the school community must help children understand core civic virtues, and must adopt, commit to, and practice them.

Our challenge is far greater today than ever before because our school populations have increased in diversity of race, languages, culture, religious belief, family wealth and education. Schools must teach children and the adult community to adopt common civic virtues. Good character and virtuous behavior are essential to the preservation of democracy.

CHARACTER EDUCATION
MANDATES: TUESDAYS AT 2:00 P.M.

School violence incidents in Littleton, Colorado, and elsewhere throughout the United States created a renewed sense of urgency about building character in our children. Most states now mandate character education in some form or another; therefore, most schools are required to teach it. Mandates foster compliance, not commitment. Teachers and administrators often see character education as one more thing that they must jam into an already crowded curriculum.

Many schools pay lip service to building character. Character education is not embraced; it is tolerated. We often teach character education on "Tuesdays at 2:00 p.m." The lesson lasts for a half hour, and is usually followed by dismissal where our children quickly demonstrate that they haven't learned a thing. Whether Tuesdays at 2:00 p.m. or Thursdays at 11:00 a.m., students quickly perceive that this character stuff is not something about which anyone feels a strong commitment.

As we have discussed previously in this book, any innovation used to promote character must be designed with consideration of the school's culture, its current reality, and the district's vision for graduates. The theories, methods, and tools necessary to implement character education must be practiced by the entire school community.

Most importantly, evidence that measures the effectiveness of the character education system must be monitored. In short, if our character education programs were successful, student behavior would change for the better, and anti-bullying programs would be unnecessary.

Ironically, schools do not lack programs purporting to teach character. Many of these programs, like those purporting to reduce bullying, are reactions to social pressures. Schools spend enormous sums of money on these programs with little evidence that they are working. In fact, by most accounts, anti-bullying programs and zero-tolerance policies have had little to no effect on the reduction of bullying (Ihne, 2009).

Rarely do schools collect any evidence whatsoever that any of these character education programs have any sustainable affect on school culture or student behavior. All the while, students who wish to be good citizens live in fear, and, in some instances, believe that the bullies get more attention and concern than "good kids" do (Humphrey, 2008).

In many cases, bullying, date rape, teen pregnancy, cheating on tests, and steroid abuse are symptoms of poor social and emotional literacy and personal discipline. These issues are complex and interrelated. Designing, teaching, and supervising programs that embed social and emotional literacy into every phase of life at school may be the only way we will improve behavior in the school community.

CHARACTER EDUCATION IS NOT JUST FOR THE KIDS

Thomas Sergiovanni (1994) observed that schools should be communities in which the members share common bonds. The failure of schools begins with the failure of leaders to establish common bonds or values that guide a cohesive effort to build character and to encourage good citizenship within the student body and the staff.

Character education cannot be taught to the children in school unless all adults associated with the school community model the behaviors they envision for their students. The "do as I say, not as I do" concept does not work.

We accept Sergiovanni's definition of community as a collection of "individuals who are bonded together by natural will and who are together bound to a set of shared ideas and ideals. This bonding and binding is tight enough to transform them from a collection of 'I's' into a collective 'we.' As a 'we,' members are part of a tightly-knit web of meaningful relationships" (1994, p. 16).

School communities establish and support relationships for all children, especially those from poverty and those new to our culture. Additionally, schools can provide structures to meet students' basic needs. Maslow (1970) determined that safety, sense of belonging, and love were essential for the emotional development of children, and a prerequisite to academic performance.

Schools can provide a learning community "where members are committed to thinking, growing, and inquiring, and where learning is for everyone an attitude as well as an activity, a way of life as well as a process" (Sergiovanni, 1994, p. 71).

We would like to think that the vast majority of school faculty and staff are community-minded, and treat children kindly and with dignity and respect. However, we can recall a colleague or two who failed to treat students and colleagues with dignity and respect.

How often have we seen and heard administrators, teachers, aides, and secretaries screaming at kids, pointing a finger in their faces, isolating kids in the hallway, or grabbing them to gain their attention. It happens more than we would like. Frankly, once is too often.

Have you ever seen two teachers pass each other in the hallway with their classes in tow, and overhear them speak about a child in their class, who is walking no more than five feet away from them? In the worst instances, the adults treat the child as if they were invisible.

Such conversations go something like this. Mrs. Jones, her voice, dripping in sarcasm, asks her colleague,

"Hi Ms. Smith, how are *your* little *angels* today?" "Oh, Mrs. Jones, I'm having a wonderful day, with the exception of Johnny who doesn't seem able to sit still for more than two minutes and hasn't completed a shred of work all morning."

Children know what is happening. They recognize the ridicule of one child. Soon, the other children learn that ridicule is acceptable—at least when dealing with Johnny.

Frankly, this behavior is unconscionable and unacceptable—yet it happens every day in school systems throughout the country. Treating everyone with dignity and respect should be a non-negotiable behavior that is vigilantly supervised.

Concerns about the new and powerful influences on our culture like the Internet, increasingly violent and depraved behaviors reflected in video games, prime-time TV shows, and music videos have many parents, politicians, and our average citizens wondering how the school can possibly develop good character in this country. One must look beyond the external cultural phenomena in our society. Schools have an internal culture that makes a difference in the development of our students.

While school systems cannot necessarily control outside forces, effective schools influence the academic, social, and emotional behaviors that are acceptable during the time students are within schools. The culture of the school sets the stage for learning and academic achievement. Every school leader must ask if the school culture provides a safe, nurturing environment for all students and adults. If a school environment is disrespectful, filled with cliques, and promotes fear, it lacks effective moral leaders.

Sometimes, a very subtle difference exists between a socially and emotionally well-adjusted culture and one that is not healthy. Does your culture promote inquiry and dialogue among all constituents including the students? Do students have a role in school governance? Does the faculty and staff? When students in school stand up to peers or adults for an issue that is right and just, do we encourage them, ignore them, or worse, instead, discipline them? Do we actually teach them to have difficult conversations in respectful ways? What messages do we send?

Whether intentional or not, the message we send about what we actually value is transmitted through our actions. If our espoused theories about the value of social and emotional literacy misalign with our actions, the entire culture becomes dysfunctional. Dysfunction disables learning. Disabled learning yields low student performance—and violence, disrespect, and fear.

School leaders and staff have to examine themselves and determine if they are living up to the ideals of their vision and mission.

CHARACTER EDUCATION IS NOT A PROGRAM: IT IS A WAY OF BEING

Intelligence, knowledge, and learning benefit society when they are used for the advancement of social justice. Academic achievement has limited societal impact unless it is paired equally with emotional and social literacy. Inherently, schools are social systems that require their members to adhere to a social contract. In effective schools, this covenant is collectively built, commonly understood, and forms the standard by which everyone in the organization judges individual and collective behavior.

Standard-based learning that is truly meaningful develops good citizens whose knowledge applies to the good of the community.

There are literally hundreds of character education programs available in schools. Many purport to be the most effective at changing student behavior. Others make no claims about changing behavior. They seem content to simply promote and foster a desired belief system.

The key to the successful implementation of any character education program lies not in the program itself; rather, it lies in how well the faculty and staff understand the initiative and accept it. Well-prepared faculty and staff teach and model the values and virtues espoused in the character education program. They determine if it will be a viable curriculum. Almost any program will work if faculty and staff teach and model the basic tenets of the program.

VALUES VERSUS VIRTUES

One challenge facing school systems is how to initiate character education. Should schools focus on values, or virtues, or both? The choice a school makes is highly dependent upon its culture and vision. For instance, a parochial school would most likely have little trouble instituting a values-based character education program whereas a public school would most likely pursue a virtues-based approach. Why the difference? Cultural beliefs make a difference. Values are highly personal, deep-seated, and often religious or spiritual in nature. Civic virtues reflect commonly held values, and reside in the norms of the society. Often, they can be expressed in terms that almost everyone accepts, and civic virtues can be attached to them as disciplines that citizens practice.

In almost all societies, values are deeply held and highly cherished beliefs. When Bob was in Mumbai, India, in January 2009 to speak on systems that work for students in higher education at Shri M. D. Shah Mahila College of Commerce and Arts, the President of the Board of Trustees, Mr. Patel, introduced him as an American scholar who came from a country similar to India. Mr. Patel explained to the audience that America was a democracy whose people were bound together by cherished values. In America, Mr. Patel said, "the people are bound together by their belief in freedom and equality; in India, the people are bound together by three great values: respect for all life, sharing and fairness."

Values are no more relative than any other metaphor that we love and cherish. They energize many human actions. Virtues are disciplines, habits of the mind and body that provide human beings with the power to exercise their values. Aristotle identified discipline as a practice that through repetition became a custom, a way of life, a power to act, a virtue. Some virtues and values are natural social requirements for civilized society, and absolutely necessary for democracies.

Public schools, by their very definition, serve the public. As the public has become much more culturally and economically diverse, beliefs and values vary. In the public setting, virtue-based approaches to character education often work because they boil down diverse beliefs into core virtues or civic disciplines to which almost all cultures subscribe and assign value.

In public school, a virtue-based initiative finds the common ground in which all religions and cultures can take comfort. Virtually every culture and religion accepts such notions as perseverance and honesty as desirable qualities for citizens.

A virtue approach to character education allows for some variance in personal or cultural interpretation, while retaining enough elements of commonality that all children and adults find they can agree on the civic virtues to be practiced at school. Since virtues are disciplines or powers that enable human beings to achieve certain goals, they are attached to values, such as my family or my friends.

In schools, civic virtues are attached to respect, honor, duty, status, and acceptance. The students know that these cherished behaviors enable them to belong to the school and enjoy their friends. As they practice a variety of civic virtues in the service of others in school, they learn to take delight in their abilities to communicate and be valued by adults and their peers.

Based upon our research into character education programs and our own experiences with this issue in a variety of school communities, we want to present the story of one school system and a school leader who developed a character education program. The school system identified eight core virtues that all good citizens of the elementary school had to practice.

Core Virtues

Respect– Show high regard for authority, other people, self, and country. Treat others as you would want to be treated. Understand that all people have value as human beings.

Responsibility– Be accountable in word and deed. Have a sense of duty to fulfill tasks with reliability, dependability, and commitment.

Honesty– Tell the truth. Admit wrongdoing. Be trustworthy and act with integrity.

Acceptance– Endure practices or beliefs different from your own. Keep an open mind. Accept and appreciate differences, even if you do not agree. Let others be different from you. Do not require everyone to think as you do.

Perseverance– Continue your best efforts in spite of difficulties. Face obstacles with determination and patience.

Empathy– Understand and be sensitive to the feelings, thoughts and experiences of another.

Integrity– Stand for your beliefs about the concept of right and wrong. Be your best self. Resist social pressure to do things that are wrong. Show commitment, courage, and self-discipline. Walk your talk.

Humility– Recognize and accept your own talents, abilities and imperfections.

Forgiveness– Let go of angry feelings, and pardon an offense.

Compassion– Show understanding of peers. Treat them with kindness, generosity, and a forgiving spirit.

We admire the elementary school staff and leaders who achieved full school and community commitment to practice the core virtues that we described above. To understand how the school achieved this consensus we have to walk through a complex and enlightening pathway. The first part of the journey deals with an awakening sense of diversity among students and their parents.

BRIDGING AND BONDING ILLUMINATED

As schools become more culturally diverse, school leaders recognize that students tend to hang out with children of like interests, backgrounds, and cultures. There is nothing inherently wrong or bad about this. In fact, as adults, we all make the same choices. We live in communities where we feel most comfortable.

Where bonding among people of similar attributes starts to have a deleterious effect on society and on our schools is when the natural bonding between these groups becomes a dominant social structure that requires the exclusion of others as the test for bonded neighbors or students. If bonding becomes cliques and gangs, trouble brews.

The guiding idea that the United States holds dear is that of *E pluribus unum* where from many cultures, races, and religions, one free people rules. In the United States, we believe that different people may preserve their beliefs and practices as long as they respect the core American beliefs of individual freedom, equality, and the pursuit of happiness. These are the values considered essential to being an American (Huntington, 2004).

In America, after several generations, immigrant families consider themselves Americans. Sometimes they brand their Americanism in a way that reflects their heritage. They describe themselves as Irish-American, African-American, Italian-American, Mexican-American, or other sundry options that comprise American diversity.

All people need to take pride in their heritage. Our ancestry should be a source of historical pride and provide us with a resilient self-identity (Carter, 2008). We should celebrate and help children to have pride in their roots. In fact, as Americans, celebrating and accepting our diversity is a guiding idea that impacts every word in our Constitution.

Diversity is not easy to manage and celebrate in schools. School districts need policy, a constitution to manage diversity, just as our nation does. In Rich's district, when students wanted to start a new club or activity, it was incumbent upon them to find an advisor who would be willing to work with them for the first year with no compensation.

If the activity was still active after one year, it was typically funded and officially adopted as an extra-curricular offering.

One of the interesting illustrations of diverse student needs and hopes resides in a story Rich tells of the dance team. Like most high schools, his district had a Kick Line that performed with the marching band and at basketball games.

Most dance teams in the region were very competitive, and the girls who made the squad typically had taken private dance lessons before they began school. This fact alone made the dance team somewhat exclusive. Access to the dance team would be limited if your life path did not fit this profile. The cultural bias towards a middle-class high school female with prior dance experience was inherent in the dance team structure.

Rich's district was approximately 90 percent White when he began working there in 1975. By 1995, the demographic patterns had begun to shift towards greater numbers of minorities and by 2006 the student demographics had changed significantly.

The African-American and Latino populations were growing rapidly, and the White population represented approximately 78 percent of the school district's enrollment of 10,000 students.

As the student demographics in the school district changed, diverse students learned to exercise their rights. In the area of student rights, school was working.

In 2001, several African-American girls visited the high school principal and asked if they could form a Step Dancing team. When asked why they didn't try out for the existing dance team, they didn't cite the bias built into the acceptance process; rather, they simply said that the dance style adopted by the Kick Line didn't interest them.

They told the principal that they had already secured a volunteer advisor. So, in accordance with general practice in the district, the principal approached Rich in his role as superintendent and outlined how the students had followed the appeal process for a new club or activity.

Remembering the wisdom of Sergiovanni (1994), Rich and his principal discussed how to provide the bonding activity the girls desired, and how to insure that the activity was bridged to the student population as a whole. They did not want to create conflict between the dance teams. Previously, anything associated with "dance" was within the exclusive province of the Kick Line. The administrators knew that more thought and discussion would be needed to allow the newly formed Step Team the opportunity to weave its way into the school's culture.

To the credit of the girls and the wisdom of the high school principal, the leaders of both groups were brought together, apprised of the situation, and proceeded to work out all of the necessary compromises. The Step Club and the Kick Line agreed to work together, and to live in harmony. As time progressed, most members would attest that they learned routines from each other.

Of course, the Latina students had no interest in either the Kick Line or the Step Dancers. They wanted to form a Latin Dance Club. They too came forearmed with a volunteer advisor. The principal conducted the same process. Similar conversations occurred among the different dance team members and very similar results emerged.

Interestingly, though not at all surprisingly, almost eight years later these groups still thrive, and because of the purposeful bridging that was designed into the process, these groups are less about bonding along cultural or ethnic lines and more about diverse students bonding according to shared interests in music and dance.

When these three groups perform at various school events and talent shows, they all receive standing ovations. The principal led the way. Bonding and bridging were powerful concepts that the principal understood to be necessary for the development of citizens in a diverse and healthy school. The successes with these diverse students highlighted how shared values, respect, and collegiality matter in schools. The second part of our journey takes us into a larger discussion group dealing with violence at school.

ONE DISTRICT'S JOURNEY OUT OF VADIR

In an effort to reduce violence at a large, suburban school district with few fiscal resources, Rich convened a discussion group on the fulfillment of the district mission. The group reviewed academic data as well as discipline referral data and the report required by New York State called the VADIR (Violence and Discipline Incidence Report). The group determined that there was a gross misalignment between the academic, social, and emotional behaviors that the district desired and what the student behavior data revealed.

Despite the best efforts of faculty and staff, the district had stagnated on increasing student achievement, and failed in its effort to reduce discipline referrals district-wide. The good news was that the district had made strong progress moving struggling learners to proficiency, and most of the discipline referrals were not for egregious crimes like assault or weapons possession.

However, administrators were spending too much time dealing with discipline referrals, and too little time supervising instruction.

The research clearly established a link between administrators unable to supervise instruction and academic stagnation. The more discipline administrators managed, the less time they had to supervise instruction, and the less impact they had on student achievement (see Figure 7.1). Rich needed to address this situation. He felt very strongly that the root cause for academic mediocrity and poor behavior was the lack of social and emotional literacy displayed throughout the school system (Goleman, 2006).

It should be noted that every school in Rich's district followed state mandates for character education. The district wanted to develop authentic

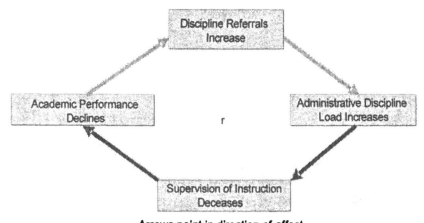

Arrows point in direction of affect.
Light grey arrows = positive affect   Dark grey arrows = declining affect

Figure 7.1.

learning communities, increase opportunities for children to learn, and increase good behavior and reduce student misbehavior. During the course of several weeks, Rich asked for more data, and had conversations with multiple constituent groups. Their input was sought about what they knew about social and emotional literacy and its connection to academic achievement.

The first finding of importance was that everyone agreed that character education was an important correlate to good behavior, and time to implement it was very limited. Second, school personnel viewed character education as another unfunded mandate required by the State. It was not attached to social and emotional literacy. Third, there was a lack of understanding about social and emotional literacy. Specifically, school leaders and teachers did not know that social and emotional literacy was a predictor of success in life and academic performance (Goleman, 1995, 2006).

In order to refocus the district's efforts on social and emotional literacy, Rich created a cross-disciplinary team to research social and emotional literacy. To demonstrate the importance and urgency of this work, the superintendent served as an "ex-officio" member of the team. The work included a mixture of inquiry and direct instruction.

The first step of the journey was to form a research committee. Through invitation, five teachers and administrators volunteered to work on this project. They were not paid a stipend. The committee consisted of two elementary assistant principals, a middle school assistant principal, and two social workers.

The team brought both depth and a wide range of experience and knowledge to this task. The "team" was deeply committed to this work. They had the ability to work and learn together. Their collective capacity to learn, as well as their knowledge of the district, enabled them to collect and share their findings within the metaphor of character education and its connection to student achievement.

They were experienced educators in this district. Two committee members were elementary assistant principals; one had over twenty years experience as an intermediate-level elementary educator in a variety of districts. The other had over twenty years' teaching experience in kindergarten, first and fourth grade in Rich's district. The middle school assistant principal was formerly a health instructor in the district. One social worker was employed by the district and knew the clientele and school culture well. The other social worker represented a local Board of Cooperative Education Service program dealing with anti-bullying strategies in the district.

One of the assistant principals, Dr. Deborah DeLuca, became coordinator of the committee's work. All participants understood the inquiry-based leadership and learning model, systems thinking, and how to build authentic learning communities. They possessed a deep commitment to this work.

The first task was to research "character education" and "social and emotional literacy." Once everyone had a clear concept of what "good character" was and how social and emotional literacy was developed in schools, they created a design that called for an open approach to character education in each school. In this effort, they were guided by prior knowledge of the faculty, site-based management teams at each school, and very strong parent groups at each school.

They wanted the end product to provide guidance to every constituent on what the district valued, and how the domain of social and emotional literacy would be assessed. The guidelines they developed allowed every school to choose its own method of meeting the goals set forth in the guidance document for character education. In this way, each school could customize a character education approach or program to its needs. The unifying factors district-wide were to be a set of guiding ideas and producing evidence of their success.

CREATING A VISION FOR CHARACTER EDUCATION FOCUSED UPON CORE VIRTUES

True to all new initiatives, a vision statement specific to this task needed to be created and aligned to the district's vision and mission. After almost a year-long focus on research and best practices, the group had sufficient knowledge and understanding to begin developing the vision statement for character education. Central to their research, and heavily influencing their vision, were the core virtues that would form the building blocks of social and emotional literacy.

The statement below represents the vision statement that the committee agreed upon, and in which they specifically referenced the social and emotional literacy project.

The School District is an active learning community of students, parents, educators, and staff. We are committed to developing responsible citizens who demonstrate virtuous behaviors through the awareness, reflection, teaching, and internalizing of *core virtues.*

Our vision will be achieved through all constituent groups participating in continuous growth and personal mastery of *core virtues* that provide the social and emotional literacy necessary for academic success and responsible citizenship.

The statement about the core virtues aligned with the district's mission. The character education statement expanded upon the themes cited in the mission. Thus, the character education program with its emphasis on social and emotional literacy was part of the district mission.

GUIDING IDEAS FOR THE CHARACTER EDUCATION PROGRAM

Once a vision statement was designed and adopted, guiding ideas were created to further define and clarify the vision. Criteria for success and evidence of progress were identified. This is a critical phase in the process.

As the deep understanding of social and emotional literacy and best practices in character education grew among planners and staff members in the research stage of this process, the character education initiative began to take shape. The guiding ideas that the committee developed expressed the basic beliefs that the staff would be asked to adopt.

The committee proposed these guiding ideas for character education at each school:

- We believe that social and emotional literacy is necessary for academic success.
- We believe responsible citizenship is developed through the teaching and learning of core virtues and skills of character development.
- We believe that all virtuous behavior is learned.
- We believe that students will demonstrate the capacity to reflect on their behaviors through the lens of the core virtues and generate multiple strategies to correct and model appropriate behaviors.

These guiding ideas formed the fundamental beliefs upon which the operational phase of the character education initiative was built. Although each school building was free to select its own means of providing character education, the program had to align with the core beliefs and guiding ideas. The guiding ideas were broad statements that allowed a wide range of approaches to be selected. At the same time, they were specific enough to guide the initiation of a character education program centered upon social and emotional development.

BRINGING SOCIAL AND EMOTIONAL LITERACY TO LIFE

Using guiding ideas as the basis for operating principles, the committee began to further define the characteristics and behaviors associated with operations. By placing the guiding ideas into "if-then" statements, they provided the guidance that the new initiative required.

The operating principles are presented below as examples of the quality of thinking effective committees must achieve to launch a new initiative:

If we believe that social and emotional literacy is necessary for academic success then . . .

- We must teach and empower students and adults to think, feel, and act guided by our core virtues: respect, responsibility, and integrity.
- All students and adults must create and model behaviors that contribute to the physical, social, and emotional health of our school community.

If we believe responsible citizenship is developed through the teaching and learning of core virtues and skills of character development then . . .

- Adults and students must know and comprehend each core virtue.
- Adults and students will internalize the knowledge gained through the study of our core virtues.
- Adult and student actions will demonstrate the application of these core virtues.
- Core virtues will be embedded into all curricula (what), the pedagogy (how), and counseling and management practices.

If we believe that all virtuous behavior is learned, then . . .

- All constituent groups demonstrate a common vocabulary and understanding of virtuous behaviors.
- All adults must create opportunities for students that allow them to reflect and analyze their behavior through the lens of our core virtues.

If we believe that students will demonstrate the capacity to reflect on their behaviors through the lens of the core virtues, and generate multiple strategies to correct and model appropriate behaviors, then . . .

- We will ensure that all understand, support and model our shared vision of student success.
- Adults and students need to understand the constructs of virtuous behavior.

As with most change initiatives, the actual process was more fluid and organic in nature, and not as linear as the list above seems to indicate. Feedback from a variety of constituents in the community, the unions, and the staff, parents, and students was essential to the successful planning and delivery of the new system for character education.

Appropriate inclusion of constituent feedback is typical of work accomplished by a knowledgeable, reflective community of learners like this design committee. When feedback was required, it was obtained in a variety of ways, both informally and formally. With feedback in hand at each meeting, the vision and guiding ideas were continually refined and clarified.

By keeping the conversation alive, more issues were brought to the surface for consideration and clarification. The open feedback process helped to refine the final initiative. New learning was easily incorporated into the design of the curriculum before the new character education initiative was rolled out publicly.

Notice: the district did not design a "program." The committee offered a set of guidelines and expectations to guide the program. Character education had to be implemented at each school by the school leaders, teachers, parents, staff, and students. This approach encouraged creativity and custom-design approaches that best suited each school's culture and capacity to change. Each school developed a character education "program" that followed the tenets set forth in the vision and guiding ideas.

THE DISTRICT DEBUT OF CHARACTER EDUCATION

In all actuality, the district's "debut" of this initiative was somewhat anti-climactic. As with all successful initiatives, the process was transparent, and team members frequently provided updates to faculties and the administration. Parents, Parent/Teacher Organizations, teacher union representatives and community groups participated in open forums to develop the character education program. The developmental process was transparent, and was open to all constituents.

The major goal of the "official roll-out" was to set context for this initiative, explain the overall process, the vision, guiding ideas, and the operating principles. This stage was critical to establish common understanding and "buy-in" among all stakeholders. This stage was not rushed, and ample time for discussion at each school was provided.

The entire process described above, including the time spent researching social and emotional literacy and best practices, took almost one and a half years. By being thorough, accessing regular feedback from multiple constituent groups, and continually refining the committee's *Character Education Resource Guide,* the research and design team effectively set the stage for a successful implementation of this initiative.

The district did not mandate a program for implementation district-wide. Rather, the district explicitly stated schools had options to choose any program they wished, even those they were currently using. The district required schools to demonstrate alignment with the vision, guiding ideas, and instructional practices expected for character education. Because of the autonomy and local choice option for each school, the "push-back" normally associated with change initiatives was minimized.

Choice is an important facet of adult learning theory, and was a purposeful part of the design in this change effort.

As anyone knows who served as a school principal, the success of the program was in the hands of school building leaders. After teaching building leaders the conceptual and practical frameworks that the character education program was built upon, the committee acted as a resource for every school. The district office accepted the role of supervising and helping building leaders develop faculty and staff capacity to present, practice and inculcate social and emotional literacy as part of character education.

ONE SCHOOL'S JOURNEY TO CORE VIRTUES

At one school, the school leaders invited all faculty and staff to voluntarily participate in a character education study group. The "Character in Action" team (C.I.A.) was well represented at each grade level including support personnel and special-area teachers. In fact, approximately thirty of the school's seventy teachers initially volunteered to join the team. Participation on this committee was without pay, a culturally accepted practice in this district. Teachers could volunteer for committees at their school.

The first impulse of the teachers was to create assembly programs, banners, and the like before everyone possessed a deep understanding of the guiding ideas and the intended outcomes. The leader's challenge was to redirect the faculty effort from superficial banners to a deep understanding of the changes the district wanted in student and professional behavior.

The assistant principal led the team's initial meeting by reviewing and deconstructing the meaning of each guiding idea in the handbook on character education. This allowed her school community to understand the guiding ideas deeply, and develop common vocabulary and definitions for the concepts they contained.

The process of understanding the guiding ideas took almost four months. The delicate and careful inquiry into the meanings underlying the handbook led to faculty enthusiasm for both the importance of this work as well as a desire to start implementation immediately.

Once the guiding ideas were embraced, the staff underwent a process of deconstructing each core virtue and creating common understandings of how each virtue was defined. They had to envision how the virtues would materialize in student and staff behavior if actualized in their school community.

According to Assistant Principal, Deborah DeLuca: "One of the tools I used to develop these concepts in my community was a model taught to us by Richard Strong at a Superintendent's Conference Day in 2004 that helped to reinforce deep learning. We collectively learned the common vocabulary and definitions of each virtue. We learned to draw a picture of what each would look like and what it would not look like. Everyone eventually held the same vision of success."

Strong's (2004) strategies helped teachers learn the guiding ideas and core virtues. Aside from the common understanding and a unified picture of what success looked like, the assistant principal was actually modeling a strategy that was later widely used by teachers to help their students learn the core virtues and how they applied to them personally.

Sincere efforts were made by school leaders to explicitly clarify for students and adults how the core virtues applied to their interactions with each other within the greater school community.

Naturally, these lessons were applicable to life at home also. Parents commented how shocked they were at first when their children started to express their disappointment if a parent failed to treat them with dignity and respect at home.

We recall fondly a mother of a kindergartener who informed the Assistant Principal that the school had done a terrific job teaching the core virtues. Her son, who was learning to tie his shoes, admonished her for teasing him as he struggled to tie his laces. He told her that she was not treating him with respect and he had learned in school that "he wouldn't be mean to her if she was having difficulty trying to learn something new."

In another district, where character education was part of the total curricula, we learned from a principal how a first grade teacher told her: "I had my lesson in character education this morning when I raised my voice to Thomas. Little Tamara looked at me and said: 'Is that a nice way to show respect for someone else?'"

We enjoy hearing these stories because they confirm that character education has become part of the social and emotional literacy of the school. As Robert Coles (1992) suggested in the *Call of Stories,* the stories we tell translate our values and beliefs about what is important in our culture.

In the development of a deep understanding of civic virtues for schools, we suggest that the pathway to follow is quite simple and very direct: define the virtue, state what it is and what it is not, practice the virtue and recognize its value. An example for humility follows:

Define the Virtue:
Humility is the ability to recognize and accept my own imperfection. Without humility I cannot pursue my own improvement.
What does it look like? What can it enable me to do?
Humility enables me to self-assess, reflect on my personal and academic goals. It allows for self-improvement, quality, and excellence.
What does it not look like? What does it prevent?
Humility prevents arrogance, bigotry, and mediocrity.
What activities can a classroom teacher (or buildings) do to promote this virtue?
Have students evaluate their work, set their goals, show evidence when they have met their goal. Let students demonstrate growth in a developmental portfolio that includes reflection sheets. Teach the students to engage in dialogue and lead with inquiry.

In the school we used as our example of character education, they used the inquiry process for every single virtue. Obviously, depending on the grade level, the teachers used definitions for virtues that were developmentally appropriate. They also began to collect materials that illustrated each virtue, sometimes explicitly and sometimes not.

The school librarian used the electronic catalogues to further refine this task so that a teacher could request books within a child's area of interest and reading level that addressed a particular virtue such as perseverance. This process of interdisciplinary collaboration reinforced and illustrated how one of our operating principles, "embedding the core virtues into curriculum and pedagogy," could be easily managed.

The school in our example did not choose to implement a character education "program." Rather, they focused on bringing the core virtues to life in their school and among all members of their school community. To further promote confidence among the faculty and staff, they decided to deeply teach one virtue each month until all virtues were taught. While the core virtues remained the same each year, the children's understanding and interpretation matured as they grew.

A VAST ARRAY OF TOOLS ARE DEPLOYED

The school participated in "Project Wisdom (1992)." After morning announcements and the Pledge of Allegiance, the "Daily Words of Wisdom" were read over the public address system by students or by an adult. This program provided quotes or small vignettes that had "thought-provoking, inspirational messages," that aligned nicely with the core virtues.

Parent newsletters were also customary and all featured a message from the principal that created common understandings about the "Virtue of the Month." The principal also recommended additional readings and strategies for parents to use with their children at home to reinforce their understandings of the virtues.

School community meetings with students of different grade levels occurred in the library once a month, and every grade level had their own meeting. In her role as a principal, Dr. DeLuca used "town meetings" for students to introduce each new "Virtue of the Month." She read a story appropriate for each grade level that incorporated the virtue of the month, and then she led a discussion of the virtue with students.

She helped them create their own picture of what the virtue meant and what it didn't mean. She reported: "Every meeting was designed to be developmentally relevant to each grade level, yet similarities emerged. For instance, after reading and discussing a story I would always end by asking the children to provide examples of how they might demonstrate the virtue in their classrooms, the hallway, the student dining room, the playground, on the bus, and at home."

CREATING ALIGNMENT

During the subsequent three school years, the results of the character education program in this school were measurable quantitatively as well as qualitatively. When students were sent to the office to see the principal for discipline, they were expected to explain their offending behavior in the context of the core virtues, and to reflect upon how their actions offended another classmate or teacher within the community. Before leaving the office, students were asked to express at least six other ways they could have modified their behavior so that they were supportive of their classmates and the entire school community. Naturally, they were expected to use the language and concepts contained in the core virtues.

Initially, a behavioral rubric was designed and employed by many staff members, mostly in the intermediate grade levels, to guide disciplinary interventions. By year two of this initiative, it was rarely used. It was no longer needed. Behavior shifted dramatically towards good citizenship and self discipline.

Even the hallways were renamed to align with the core virtues. The hallway outside Kindergarten classrooms was called Compassion Court. There was also Perseverance Place, Respect Road, and the hall outside the principal's office was called Forgiveness Fairway. Cute is rarely effective unless it also counts. These metaphors and symbolic names met the test of being both cute and purposeful since behavioral results were monitored and celebrated.

SUPERVISING TO THE GUIDING IDEAS

We have touched upon the importance of leaders modeling the behavior they wish to see among their faculty, staff, and students. In turn, teachers must model the behaviors they expect from their peers and students. In the vernacular, everyone has to "walk their talk." Of course, every once in a while someone stumbles. When they do, they need to be brought back into the fold.

Whether disciplining students or employees, a school leader must be forthright and be fair. Everyone should be treated with dignity and given respect, even when it was not earned. Supervision should address the expected standards for professional behavior.

When tenured faculty and staff members are not aligned with the core virtues, they should be confronted privately and directly, and expectations for their behavior or performance should be explicitly stated and documented. Everyone should expect that expectations will be supported by the school leaders and supervised closely and corrected when necessary. The overarching message is simple. Supervise the desired initiatives and behaviors. There is a far greater likelihood that the district vision will be fulfilled if school leaders ensure there is a proper execution of the endeavor.

EVIDENCE

Evidence of success comes in many forms. One of Rich's favorite stories that bespeaks of the success of the social and emotional literacy initiative occurred one day when a school principal asked a youngster, who exhibited symptoms of autism, to discuss the virtue of the month. This youngster proceeded to discuss, in great detail, what the virtue of that month was and how it was modeled. Without prompting, he named the month's virtue "perseverance," and reminded the principal of all of the other virtues he had learned that year. He proceeded to name all of the other virtues in the order that they had practiced them that year. His mother and teacher received a letter of commendation from the principal as did the student.

The story is an example of qualitative evidence. Sometimes, a series of stories such as the one above provides evidence that the culture has shifted to a desired result. The more the stories change and align with the vision held for character education, the more the culture embraces the change. When the "old" stories virtually disappear or are referenced with an air of incredulity, a new culture *has taken shape*.

Finally, for our readers who are hesitant to consider character education at the level of importance that we assign to it, we want to share the 2004–2005 school year baseline data for student disciplinary referrals at this school. Witness the dramatic improvements wrought under the character education initiative.

DISCIPLINE DECLINES AS SELF DISCIPLINE GROWS

At this elementary building, a discipline report was filed with the office by a teacher, teacher assistant, or paraprofessional who believed that a student's behavior needed to be addressed by the assistant principal or principal. In 2004–2005, before the character education program had been implemented, there were 161 reports filed with the office. In 2005–2006, the number of reports dropped to 125. During 2006–2007, there were six discipline reports to the office.

During the 2004–2005 school year there were nineteen student suspensions from school. During 2005–2006, there were twenty-two suspensions. In 2006- 2007, there were four suspensions.

In this district, a bus report is filed by the bus driver if a student demonstrates unsafe or inappropriate behavior on the school bus. The improvement noted in the school building did not translate from the first to second year on the school buses. The number of bus reports in 2004–2005 was 163. There were 214 bus reports in the 2005–2006, an increase of fifty-one reports. During 2006–2007, the school saw a remarkable drop in bus reports. There were thirty-seven bus reports that year. What changed?

The school leaders realized they had not involved the bus drivers in the dialogue about school virtues. Once the bus drivers understood the virtues and the key words referencing each virtue, they were able to use them to call for student attention to good character and virtuous, disciplined behavior. Of course, their principal and teachers expected these virtues would be practiced outside the school as well.

Correcting that oversight with the bus drivers accounted for the drop in bus reports in 2006–2007. The changes in student behavior on the buses illustrate how difficult it is for children to transfer learned behavior in one setting to another setting unless it is modeled, expected and taught by the entire school community.

ACADEMIC GAINS

By the 2006–2007 school year, 90 percent of the students exited kindergarten reading on or above grade level. The same trend happened in first grade and continued into second grade. The gains at each level carried through and were built upon at every successive grade level. The number of students performing at the lowest levels of 1 and 2 literacy levels began to diminish markedly as formative assessment data used to inform and monitor student reading progress improved. As student behavior improved in the classrooms, teachers were able to dedicate more time to differentiated instruction.

Most impressive was that the performance gaps between disaggregated groups of ethnic students diminished. Socioeconomic status and race or ethnicity became less and less accurate predictors of academic failure.

UNANTICIPATED CONSEQUENCES

The unanticipated consequences of the focus on core virtues were also positive. School attendance, in 2007, for students and teachers exceeded 94 percent. Internal complaints as well as external complaints about anything and everything dropped dramatically. Parent participation in school-related activities grew during this time, as did their support for the school.

According to the school principal, Dr. DeLuca: "The most important thing that happened, along with the positive shift in academic gains, was that the mental models of students and teachers shifted. At the outset of our initiative, teacher conferences about students focused on student deficits. As we progressed in character education, teacher comments focused on student strengths. Interestingly, everyone began to see potential in everything we did where before they only saw barriers to success."

SYSTEMS THAT WORK FOR STUDENTS

Character education imbedded in a social and emotional literacy program at a school and practiced daily by all employees and students with the support of parents makes an important contribution to systems that work for students. School leaders who want to make a difference for students and help them become successful adults should adopt a model character education program as we suggest.

Curricula should be organized in ways that expected student performance levels are clear, expansive, measurable, and observable. Students should be expected to demonstrate creative and critical thinking, to show empathy, interpretative skills, to dramatize and express insight into a variety of exploratory adventures in math, science, social science, and the arts.

Teacher supervision should be characterized by a dialogue infused with inquiry, exploration and accountability. Respected professionals should come together at the school and diagnose, prescribe, and promote a healthy learning community for teachers, school leaders, parents, and students.

Students should be engaged in challenging cognitive activities and social and emotional roles that help them to acquire leadership and collaborative skills.

School leaders must practice the virtues of effective visionaries. They need to acquire the patience to develop relationships. They need to be open to challenges to their mental models. They need to develop self-discipline, persistence and patience which fuel constructive change in a school system.

Valued and trusted feedback, from a variety of sources, and well-researched strategies should guide all actions and decisions of administrators. Teachers, parents and students should have many ways to participate in the life of the school and in the decision-making process. Leadership opportunities should be shared. Thoughtful school leaders should be designing small systems inside the school that promote creative leadership opportunities for many teachers, students and parents. The greater the diversity of planned leadership within a school, the higher the productivity every student exhibits.

In closing, we would like to state that the systems that work for students are:

Curriculum Design and Implementation Focused on Student Performance
School and District Leadership Infused with Systems Thinking
Diagnostic and Prescriptive Skills Focused on Strengths
Engaged Students in Social, Emotional, and Cognitive Development
Systems Analysis, Continuous Improvement, Inquiry, and Dialogue
Effective School Board Governance
Character Education

References

Argyris, C., and Schön, D. 1978. *Organizational learning: A theory of action perspective.* Reading, MA: Addison Wesley.

Baldwin, R., and Hughes, J. T. 1995. *Boards at their best; A new approach toward improved board effectiveness* (1st ed.). New York: Educational Consulting Associates and Connolly-Cormack.

Bennis, W. B. 1997. *Managing people is like herding cats.* Provo, UT: Executive Excellence Publishing.

Bennis, W. B. and P. W. Biederman. 1997. *Organizing genius: The secrets of creative collaboration.* Reading, MA: Addison-Wesley.

Bennis, W. B., T. G. Cummings, and G. M. Spreitzer. 2001. (Eds) *The future of leadership.* San Francisco: Jossey-Bass, A Wiley Company.

Bennis, W. 1999. *Old dogs, new tricks.* Provo, UT: Executive Excellence Publishing.

Blake, P. M. 2007. Head's of charter schools attitudes toward autonomy, instructional leadership, sense of community, climate of continuous systematic improvement, and their student academic proficiency in grade eight. EdD diss., Dowling College. *Dowling College database*, publ. nr. AAT 3272788.

Bloom, Benjamin S. 1981. *All Our Children Learning.* New York: McGraw Hill Book Company.

Bloom, B. S., and Krathwohl, D. R. (1956). *Taxonomy of educational objectives: The classification of educational goals by a committee of college and university examiners. Handbook 1: Cognitive Domain.* New York: Longmans.

Bolton, J. E. 2005. The relationship among school business administrator's actual and ideal use of computer technology and school financial efficiency. EdD diss., Dowling College. *Dowling College database*, publ. nr. AAT 3272788.

Bossert, K. 2008. A comparative analysis of the influence of high stakes teasting mandates in the elementary school. EdD diss., Dowling College. *Dowling College database*, publ. nr. AAT 3317859.

Burak, M. 2006. Governance practices, teamwork, effectiveness, and curriculum responsibilities in urban and suburban school board members in the northeast region of the United States. EdD diss., Dowling College. *Dowling College database,* publ. nr. AAT 3222090.

Burns, J. M. 1978. *Leadership* (1st ed.). New York: Harper and Row.

Cafferty, J. 2009. CNN Commentary(April)

Callahan, R. E. 1962. *Education and the cult of efficiency: A study of the social forces that have shaped administration of the public schools.* Chicago: University of Chicago Press.

Caputo, L. 2004. A case study of student perceptions of the ethic of care among educators in a Long Island high school. EdD diss., Dowling College. *Dowling College database,* publ. nr. AAT 3173569.

Carr, C. G. 2004. The relationship of New York State school board members' attitudes of importance and existence of eight governance competencies developed by the National School Board Association. EdD diss., Dowling College. *Dowling College database,* publ. nr. AAT 3149867.

Carter, D. J. (Fall 2008). Achievement as resistence: The development of a critical race achievement ideology among black achievers. *Harvard Educational Review,* v78, n.3 pp. 466–497.

Carter, S. C. 2001. *No excuses: Lesson from 21 high-performing, high-poverty schools.* Washington, DC: The Heritage Foundation.

Carver, J. 1997. *Boards that make a difference: A new design for leadership in nonprofit and public organizations.* San Francisco: Jossey-Bass Publishers.

Carver, J. 2000. Toward coherent governance. *The School Administrator,* 57(3):6–10.

Chait, R. P., T. P. Holland, and B. E. Taylor. 1996. *Improving the performance of governing boards.* Phoenix: Oryx Press.

Chen, J. A. 2003. *The role of school boards, their governance practices and sense of effectiveness in suburban, urban, and rural settings in the United States.* UMI: Ann Arbor.

Christie, J. 2009. Teacher Perception of the Implementation of Middle-level Program Components, Their Attitude Toward No Child Left Behind and Instructional Practice Related to Test Preparation in High, Middle, and Low Need Middle Schools. EdD diss., Dowling College.

Coles, R. 1989. *The call of stories: Teaching and the moral imagination.* Boston: Houghton Mifflin.

Collins, J. 2001. *Good to great.* New York: Harper Collins Publishers.

Connell, J. P., M. B. Spencer, and J. L. Aber. 1994. Educational risk and resilience in African American youth: Context, self, action, outcomes in school. *Child Development,* 65:493–506.

Cottrell, D. 2002. *Monday morning leadership.* Dallas: Cornerstone Leadership Institute.

Danielson, C. 2007. *Enhancing professional practice: A framework for teaching.* Alexandria, VA: Association for Supervision and Curriculum Development.

Darling-Hammond, L. 1998. Foreword to *What's worth fighting for out there?* by A. Hargreaves, and M. Fullan. (Eds.) New York: Teachers College Columbia University.

Deal, T. E., and K. D. Peterson. 1999. *Shaping school culture: The heart of leadership.* San Francisco: Jossey-Bass.

Deci, E. L. and R. M. Ryan. 2000. The "what" and "why" of goal pursuits: Human needs and self determination of behavior. *Psychological Inquiry* 11:227–268.

DeLuca, D., and R. J. Hawkins. 2007. Character education: An elementary school's journey toward implementing a virtue-based, systemic program that emphasizes dignity and respect among all stakeholders. Paper presented at the Dowling College 2nd Annual Research Symposium, New York.

Deming, W. Edwards. 1982, 1986. *Out of crisis.* Cambridge, MA: Massachusetts Institute of Technology, Center for Advanced Engineering Study.

Deming, W. Edwards. 1994. *The new economics.* Cambridge, Massachusetts: Massachusetts Institute of Technology, Center for Advanced Engineering Study.

Eisenberg, C. 2004. New York State school board members' attitude towards school governance, financial practices, conflict, teamwork and board effectiveness. EdD diss., Dowling College. Ann Arbor, MI UMI Dissertation Services.

Feltman, J. A. 2003. The relationship between four components of governance and coercive power among school board trustees in selected Suffolk County, New York school districts. EdD diss., Dowling College. *Dowling College database,* publ. nr. AAT 3094782.

Finn, J. D., and K. E. Voelkl. 1993. School characteristics related to student engagement. *Journal of Negro Education* 62(3):249–268.

Friedman, T. L. 2006. *The world is flat: A brief history of the twenty-first century.* New York: Farrar, Straus and Giroux.

Fullan, M. 2001. *Leading in a culture of change.* San Francisco: Jossey-Bass.

Fulton, T. 2009. A comparison of high school teacher perceptions of their principal's instructional behavior in high and low needs schools. EdD diss., Dowling College.

Furrer, C., E. and Skinner. 2003. Sense of relatedness as a factor in children's academic engagement and performance. *Journal of Educational Psychology* 95(1):148–162.

Gates, W., N. Myhrvold, and P. Rinearson. 1996. *The road ahead.* New York: Viking Press.

Gest, S. D., J. A. Welsh, and Domitrovich. 2005. Behavioral predictors of changes in social relatedness and liking school in elementary school. *Journal of School Psychology* 43(4):281–301.

Gladwell, M. 2008. *Outliers: The story of success.* New York: Little, Brown and Company.

Golman, D. 1995. *Emotional intelligence: Why it can matter more than IQ.* New York: Bantam.

Golman, D. 2007. *Social intelligence: The revolutionary new science of human relationships.* New York: Bantam.

Goodenow, C. 1992. School motivation, engagement, and sense of belonging among urban adolescent students. Paper presented at the annual meeting of American Educational Research Association, San Francisco, California, April 20–24.

Goodenow, C. 1993. Classroom belonging among early adolescent students: Relationships to motivation and achievement. *Journal of Early Adolescence* 13:21–43.

Goodman, R. H., and W. G. Zimmerman, Jr. 2000. *Thinking differently: Recommendations for 21st century school board/superintendent leadership, governance, and teamwork for high student achievement.* Arlington, VA: The New England School Development Council and Educational Research Service.

Graves, R. 1990. (ed.) *Rhetoric and composition: A sourcebook for teachers and writers.* Portsmith, NH: Boyton and Smith.

Grimaldi, M. 2009. The academic achievement and engagement of non-disabled male and female students educated within middle level inclusive and general education classrooms. EdD diss., Dowling College.

Grucci, C.R. 2004. Executive team stability and school board members' attitudes towards school finance and governance practices in selected Nassau County, Long Island, New York school districts. EdD diss., Dowling College. *Dowling College database*, publ. nr. AAT 3114298.

Hawkins, R. J. 2003. *The relationship of team learning and the four components of school governance among school board members in Suffolk County, New York.* Ann Arbor, MI: UMI

Howell, W. G. and P. E. Peterson. 2002. *The education gap.* Washington, D.C.: The Brookings Institution.

Hargreaves, A., and D. Fink. 2006. *Sustainable leadership* (1st ed.). San Francisco: Jossey-Bass.

Hart, B. and T. Risley. 1995. *Meaningful differences in the everyday experiences of young American children.* Baltimore, MD: Paul H. Brooks Publishing Company.

Hoff, D. J. 2009. Schools struggling to meet key goal on accountability: Number failing to make AYP rises to 28 percent. *Education Week*, January.

Hoy, H. W., and C. G. Miskel. 2001. *Educational administration: Theory, research, and practice* (6th ed.). Boston: McGraw-Hill.

Hughes, J., R. Manley, and C. Rudiger. 2001. The board member as a professional: A process of self-evaluation and reflection. *Long Island Educational Review* 1(2).

Humphrey, D. 2008. *African American male gang members and non-gang members attitudes toward school in one suburban high school in Nassau County, New York.* EdD diss., Dowling College. *Dowling College database*, publ. nr. AAT 3327198.

Huntington, S. P. 2004. *Who are we? The challenges to America's national identity.* New York: Simon and Schuster.

Ihne, L. 2009. *Student character, peace education, teacher intervention to reduce student conflict, relational and cyber bullying at the middle school.* Diss., Dowling College.

Johnson, D.W. and R. T. Johnson. 2005. Essential Components of Peace Education. Theory into Practice. *ERIC* 44(4).

Kanter, R. M., B. Stein, and T. Jick. 1992. *The challenge of organizational change: How companies experience it and leaders guide it.* New York: Toronto Free Press; Maxwell Macmillan Canada; Maxwell Macmillan International.

Kennedy, J. F. 1959. Crisis and opportunity. (Publication no.) http://www.quotation-spage.com/quotes/John_F._Kennedy)

Kouzes, J. M. and B. Z. Posner. 1995. *The leadership challenge.* San Francisco: Jossey-Bass.

Leithwood, K. A., D. Jantzi, and R. Steinbach. 1999. *Changing leadership for changing times.* Buckingham; Philadelphia: Open University Press.

Lickona, T. 1991. *Educating for character: How our schools can teach respect and responsibility.* New York: Bantam Books. New York Center for School Safety. Retrieved January 28, 2007, from http://www.mhric.org/scss/save2.

Manley, R. J., L. Bishop, J. Manley, K. Turnow, and M. Manieri. 2002. *Professionalism among boards of education in Suffolk County, New York, USA.* Paper presented at the Sixth Oxford Conference for Social Issues.

Marzano, R. J. 2003. *What works in schools.* Alexandria, VA: ASCD Publication.

Marzano, R. J., D. J. Pickering, and J. E. Pollock. 2001. *Classroom instruction that works.* Alexandria, VA: ASCD Publication.

Mauro, A. 2006. *The relationship of governance to effectiveness and board development among school board members in Suffolk County, New York.* Ann Arbor, MI: UMI.

Maslow, A. 1970. *Motivation and personality.* New York: Harper Collins.

McGregor, D. 1960. *The human side of enterprise.* New York: McGraw-Hill.

McNeely, C., and C. Falci. 2004. School connectedness and the transition into and out of health-risk behaviors among adolescents: A comparison of social belonging and teacher support. *Journal of School Health* 74(7):284–292.

Moe, T. M. 2001. *Schools, vouchers and the American public.* Washington, D.C.: The Brookings Institute.

Morrissey, M. S. 2000. *Professional learning communities: An ongoing exploration.* Austin: Southwest Educational Development Laboratory.

Nesbitt, Richard E. 2009. Education is all in your mind. *New York Times,* Sunday Opinion, February 8.

No Child Left Behind Act of 2001, ESEA. USC 6301 107th Congress. 2001.

Obama, B. H. 2009. Inaugural address. *New York Times,* January 21.

Page, S. E. 2008. The power of diversity. *The School Administrator* 65(9).

Payne, R. 1998. *A framework for understanding poverty.* Highlands, TX: RFT Publishing.

Peterson, P. E. 2003. (Ed.) *Our schools and our future.* Stanford, CA: Hoover Institution Press Publication.

Reeves, D. 2000. *Accountability in sction: A blueprint for learning organizations.* Denver: Advanced Learning Press.

Resnick, M. 1999. Effective school governance: A look at today's practice and tomorrow's promise. *Education Commission of the States,* Denver, CO.: January.

Rosenberger, M. K. 1997. *Team leadership: School boards that work.* Lancaster, PA: Technomic.

Ruck, J. A., 2003. *School board attitudes toward effective functioning and gover-nance in Suffolk County, New York.* EdD diss., Dowling College. *Dowling College database,* publ. nr. AAT 3077245.

Ryan, K. 2003. Character education: Our high schools' missing link. *Education Week,* January 29. http://www.edweek.org/ http://www.edweek.org/ew/articles/2003/01/29/20ryan.h22.html (accessed January 27, 2007).

Salas, E., J. A. Cannon-Bowers, and E. L. Blickensderfer. 1997. (Eds.) *Enhancing reciprocity between training theory and practice: Principles, guidelines, and speci-fications.* Mahwah, NJ: Lawrence Erlbaum Associates.

Santos, C. A. 2009. Third and fourth grade teacher practices in cognitive and social/emotional development: Their student's academic self-concept and emotional/social skills moderated by students' mothers' level of education and time reading at home. Diss., Dowling College.

Schein, E. H. 1985. *Organizational culture and leadership.* San Francisco: Jossey-Bass.

Schorr, E. B. 1997. *Common purpose.* New York: Anchor Books.

Senge, P. 1990. *The fifth discipline: The art and practice of a learning organization.* New York: Currency Doubleday.

Senge, P. M. 2006. *The fifth discipline: The art and practice of a learning organiza-tion* (2nd ed.). New York: Currency Doubleday.

Senge, P., N. Cambron-McCabe, T. Lucas, B. Smith, J. Dutton, and A. Kleiner. 2000. *Schools that learn—A fifth discipline fieldbook for educators, parents, and every-one who cares about education.* New York: Doubleday.

Senge, P., C. Roberts, A. Kleiner, R. Ross, and B. Smith. 1999. *The dance of change.* New York: Currency Doubleday.

Sergiovanni, T. J. 1994. *Building community in schools* (1999 ed.). San Francisco: Jossey-Bass.

Sirin, S. 2004. Exploring school engagement of middle class African American ado-lescents. *Youth and Society* 35(3):323–340.

Slavin, R., N. L. Karweit, and N. A. Madden. 1989. *Effective programs for students at risk.* Boston: Allyn and Bacon.

Smoley, E. R., 1999. *Effective school boards: Strategies for improving school boards.* San Francisco: Jossey-Bass.

Stinson, D. W. 2006. African American male adolescents, schooling: Deficiency, rejection, and achievement. *Review of Educational Research* 76(4):477–506.

Stone, D. 1997. *Policy paradox: The art of political decision making.* New York: W. W. Norton and Company.

Stone, D. (March 13, 2000). Why we need a care movement, *The Nation,* pp. 13–15.

Strong, R. W., H. F. Silver, and M. J. Perini. 2001. *Teaching what matters most: Standards and strategies for raising student achievement.* Alexandria, VA: Association for Supervision and Curriculum Development.

Strong, R. W., 2004. *The year of metacognition.* Presented at William Floyd Superintendent's Conference Day, Mastic Beach, NY. February.

Turnow, K. 2002. *School board attitudes towards governance in eastern Suffolk County, New York.* Ann Arbor, MI: UMI

Viteritti, J. P. 1999. *Choosing equality.* Washington, D. C.: The Brookings Institute.

Walton, M. 1986. *The Deming management method.* New York: Putnam.

Weeks, D., Ph.D. 1994. *The eight essential steps to conflict resolution: Preserving relationships at work, at home, and in the community.* New York: Penguin Putnam, Inc.

Welch, J., and J. A. Byrne. 2001. *Jack: Straight from the gut.* New York: Warner Business Books.

Wheatley, M. J. 2006. *Leadership and the new science.* San Francisco: Berrett-Koehler.

Wiggins, G., and J. McTighe. 2005. *Understanding by design* (2nd ed.). Upper Saddle River, NJ: Prentice-Hall

Wiggins, G., and J. McTighe. 2007. *Schooling by design.* Alexandria, VA: ASCD.

Wills, G. 1994. *Certain trumpets: The call of leaders.* New York: Simon and Schuster.

Wilson, D. 2004. The interface of school climate and school connectedness and relationships with aggression and victimization. *Journal of School Health* 74(7): 293–299.

About the Authors

Robert J. Manley graduated from Iona College with a B.A. in Spanish Language Arts and minors in Philosophy and Education. He completed his Master of Arts degree in the Humanities at Hofstra University and his Professional Diploma and Doctor of Philosophy degrees in Educational Administration at St. John's University. He taught Spanish Language skills and served as an instructor in a New York State model Humanities Program at West Babylon High School. For twenty-one years he served in a variety of administrative positions including Assistant Principal at Babylon Jr./Sr. High School, Principal in Plainedge, Assistant Superintendent for Curriculum and Instruction and Superintendent of Schools in West Babylon, New York. He served as President of the Board of Directors for the Suffolk County Library System and the Suffolk County Organization to Promote Education.

Robert has been Associate Professor of Educational Administration, Leadership and Technology at Dowling College where he was Department Chairperson of doctoral and licensing programs for nine years. Currently, he is Professor of Educational Administration at Dowling College.

In the past six years, he has presented peer-reviewed papers at the Sixth Annual Conference on Social Issues at Oxford University, England, the World Association for Case Research and Application in Manheim, Germany, and Lucerne, Switzerland, and the Eastern Educational Research Association in Hilton Head, South Carolina, and Clearwater, Florida. In addition, he presented workshops on School Board Governance practices at the New York State School Boards Annual Convention and at the National School Boards Conference. On January 8, 2009, he presented *Systems that Work for Students in Higher Education* as Keynote Speaker at the International Symposium for

Quality in Higher Education at Shri M. D. Shah Mahila College of Arts and Commerce in Mumbai, India.

Richard J. Hawkins graduated from Hofstra University with his B.S. in Music Education. He completed his M.S. in Education and Professional Diploma in Education Leadership at Long Island University. Rich received his doctorate in Educational Administration at Dowling College. He began his teaching career in the William Floyd School District as an instrumental music teacher and later became District Coordinator of Music and Art. After his department was recognized as the Outstanding Music Program in the country by the Music Educators National Conference, Rich moved to the district office as the Assistant Superintendent for Elementary Education and Personnel. Schools under his supervision received designation as N.Y.S. Schools of Excellence and U.S.D.O.E. Blue Ribbon Schools. Rich served as Superintendent of the William Floyd School District for almost twelve years. He has served as President of the Suffolk County School Superintendents Association (SCSSA) and held various roles with the New York State Council of School Superintendents (NYSCOSS).

Since retiring from William Floyd, Rich has been serving as an Adjunct Professor in the M.A. and Ed.D. programs at Dowling College and in the M.A. program at the College of Saint Rose in Albany, NY. In addition to his adjunct work, Rich taught full time at the College of St. Elizabeth as Assistant Professor in their Ed.D. and Master's programs. In 2006, Rich formed Hawkins and Associates: Organizational Learning Consultants, and now helps leaders and their organizations reach their goals and aspirations. Over the last nine years he has had peer-reviewed papers presented at the World Association for Case Research and Application in Lucerne, Switzerland, and Manheim, Germany, the Eastern Educational Research Association in Hilton Head, South Carolina, and in the *Long Island Education Review*. Rich has made numerous presentations to the New York State School Boards Association, NYSCOSS, and the SCSSA. He has presented at Hofstra University's Social Emotional Literacy Conference and Dowling College's Annual Practical Research Symposium. He was also a keynote presenter at the U.S. Dept. of Education Safe School/Healthier Students Conference in Tysons Corner, VA.

Made in the USA
Middletown, DE
12 July 2015